# A Book of Assemblies

**DEREK WATERS** M.A.

MILLS & BOON LIMITED, LONDON

First published in Great Britain 1975 by Mills & Boon Limited,
17–19 Foley Street, London W1A 1DR.
Revised edition 1979

ISBN 0 263 06407 7

Printed in Great Britain by Thomson Litho Ltd.,
East Kilbride, Scotland.
Bound by Hunter & Foulis Ltd.,
Edinburgh.

# CONTENTS

# ACKNOWLEDGEMENTS

Most educational issues are matters of common concern. As I talked to various colleagues I became aware of the uncertainty that many of them feel about assemblies, and their need to exchange thoughts and ideas on the subject.

I would like to thank my colleagues at Boxgrove School, past and present, for our discussions about assemblies from time to time, for their kind reception of my assemblies, for their own willingness to lead assemblies, and for their imaginative use of story material, personal anecdotes and development of situations in which children could take an active part. I would like to give special thanks to Margaret Brandham for her inspired and sincere contributions to assemblies and generous assistance with musical items; to Pamela Hill, who was able to stimulate some quite remarkable improvised dramatic situations with staff and children participating during her assemblies; and to Alan Bradbury, sometime local vicar and part-time member of staff, for his imaginative treatment of pop music, relating it very much to young children.

Many friends outside the school have also helped me. John Bailey, RE Adviser in Lincolnshire; David Frayne, Rector of Caterham; David Shepherd, Bishop of Woolwich; Bernard Brailey; Eric Shegog and John Colchester, vicars of neighbouring churches; Jack Hames, St Alphege with St Peter's School, Greenwich, who gave me the chance to witness and participate, with helpers, staff and children, in his assemblies, and on frequent occasions to listen to his warm and witty remarks about the subject of assemblies with children; Hilary Robinson, who gave some remarkable demonstrations of how to involve the very youngest Deptford children (and their grandparents and others in the community); Brian Gates of Goldsmiths College; Sister Mary Aiden of Welling; Ron Griffiths of Woodmansterne School, for showing how music could play such a part in assemblies.

To all of these and many others I would like to say thank you and to say that they do not necessarily hold any of the views expressed herein.

Derek Waters

# Part 1

# NOTE FOR REVISED EDITION

I should like to record special thanks for advice and facilities at the R. E. Development Centre, 23 Kensington Square, London W.8, to the Rev. Paul Turton and Jan Dunnachie, who helped enormously in the revision of the resources lists in this new edition.

In the extensive revision of the book list, a very few out-of-print titles have been allowed to remain, as they are worth knowing about and there is a good chance that they may still be available in libraries.

D.W.

# INTRODUCTION

Of the half dozen books I have written, *A Book of Assemblies* has caused me the greatest difficulty. There were the usual problems of just what to say and how to say it. There was the struggle to approach the subject with an air of neutrality, but, try as one might, a very personal viewpoint did intrude from time to time. Perhaps the biggest problem was that whenever I went back to the manuscript after a brief interval, the situation seemed to have altered. The religious, moral and social climate in the country is changing so rapidly that to take your eyes off it for a moment is to discover later that it has moved ahead.

I began to join in school assemblies as a teacher about twenty years ago, and soon became aware of the Biblical claustrophobia that restricted almost everything one could do. There seemed to be a preoccupation with fear, prohibition and moralising that removed any possibility of enjoyment. The assembly scene was occupied by people in odd clothes who lived two thousand years ago in a distant land. It seemed to have little to do with the children who sat so docilely with me in that great brown hall. (I'm sure they wouldn't sit quite so still given the same fare today.)

It is important to be aware of the world in which we live, and to shape our school assemblies accordingly. If we want to ensure holding the children's attention, a prerequisite to understanding, we must make assemblies relevant to their lives and enjoyable. Children like a certain amount of routine in their school lives; it provides a framework in which creative and routine work can proceed. This is no excuse, however, for boring them with the same assembly form and content day by day. Let us put some imagination and energy into our assemblies, and make them more interesting, more relaxed and more informal.

The reader will find that this is not a hymn-reading-prayer recipe book. There are enough of them about already (see pages 118—124). I have made some suggestions on ways in which an assembly can be planned and carried out. I hope that readers will look with some interest at the section in which I have given detailed descriptions for assemblies. These should not be followed slavishly, but considered and adapted to suit the particular assembly situations being arranged. One can take various ingredients in large or small numbers from different sources. Use the parts with discretion, but avoid taking so many liberties with the material that you lose the point.

One is always anxious about the charge of entertainment that can arise if there is too large an element of apparent enjoyment in assemblies. It is important that there should be enjoyment in assemblies, with perhaps only a few exceptions. What am I trying to do in assemblies? I am trying to conduct a cooperative and open-ended search for truth. I don't think it is the role of the school to tell children what to believe. I think it is its role to help children to develop

> understanding, sympathy and respect for other people,
> an acute sense of right and wrong,
> independence of thought and action,
> a strong sense of community and the individual's
> responsibility to it,
> a sense of wonder about themselves and the world they
> live in, and to encourage their desire to find out more
> about it,
> and to celebrate with them the good news as a counter to
> the bad news that is so often all around us.

How can we best achieve these aims? Here are my basic recommendations.

We must try to impart understanding and insight, not to secure commitment. We must design assemblies that are credible and acceptable to Christian and non-Christian pupils and staff.

When considering assembly reform, we must involve everyone – pupils and staff. We must strive to involve the uncommitted, and remember that critical interest from everyone is better than apathy.

We live in a so-called Christian country, and it is desirable that we should occasionally explain what the Christian faith is so that pupils will at least know what they are accepting or rejecting.

We must try to promote sympathetic understanding of other

religious and racial groups so that we can learn to live together in harmony.

We must always remember that the range of interests, ability and experience will be wide, and whatever is done should be within the comprehension of all who attend.

We must not assume that every assembly is a religious one, nor follow an ecclesiastical pattern. There is a place for Christian, multi-faith and secular assemblies.

We must remember that we are seeking to influence rather than instruct, to inform rather than indoctrinate.

Many of our churches are sadly demoralised and have completely lost their hold. Faith as prescribed there seems no longer relevant to the majority of people. Many children come from homes that are apathetic towards the Christian faith, and only put their faces inside church to attend brief family ceremonies. It seems to many young people that the traditional format of hymn, prayer and reading in the school assembly presupposes their acceptance of 'all that' and a complete belief in the Christian faith. It is no wonder that they object.

Children today are encouraged not to accept anything until it is proven to be true. Science-orientated children are particularly critical of controversial matters spoken of with great certainty. Even at primary level some children have doubts about the validity of much of what they are told.

As well as large numbers of children with no religion, there are also large numbers of children who follow non-Christian faiths. We need to cater for them too. It is important to remember that even though people do not adhere to the Christian ethic, they do try to lead decent, reasonable lives. It is not good enough to treat them as though they were Christians. Let us not adopt the narrow-minded attitude expressed by Parson Thwackum in Henry Fielding's *Tom Jones:*

> When I mention religion, I mean the Christian religion, and not only the Christian religion, but the Protestant religion, and not only the Protestant religion, but the Church of England!

We must not try to take on the role of organised religion. There is a difference between the task of the school and that of the church, mosque, or synagogue.

In all schools opportunities occur for planning and full participation. A colleague of mine said that since she is the appointed head of the school, she should always lead it in worship. However, I think that we emphasise the corporate nature of the assembly by encouraging others to lead it. In this way monotony is eliminated. Even the repetitive pattern over the week or fortnight can be avoided by employing the various permutations of teachers, visiting speakers, and children in groups or classes. In such a plan, spontaneity and interest are reasonably assured. The daily dilemma of what to do in assembly is no longer the burden of one head teacher who may not have been appointed for his ability to hold 500 children spellbound on 200 days of every year. The use of different personalities and a variety of voices and approaches to worship and assembly go a long way towards ensuring attention, which is a prerequisite of all understanding.

I know how refreshing it is to have a new face at the front of the assembly. On each occasion that we have tried this, the assembly has been conducted extraordinarily well, even by inexperienced staff in their first year of teaching. They have invariably been apprehensive - indeed, it would be strange if they had not been. There can be few people who consider themselves adequately qualified to lead assemblies, as there is certainly no training for such work in our programme. What we need is caring and informed enthusiasts to organise our assemblies, and there are usually several of these on any staff.

You might consider it unnecessary to have an assembly every day, and better to concentrate your efforts on fewer occasions in the week. By doing this, the event should seem more significant to children.

You might also try grouping the children for assembly. Let us take as an example a two-form-entry primary school with one hall and at least one large classroom in addition to the usual accommodation. A small gathering could use the large classroom, but a share of the hall time would be needed for groups of more than eighty. The pattern might run like that on the table opposite.

12

| Day | Age group | No. of children | Venue | Time | Music | In charge |
| --- | --- | --- | --- | --- | --- | --- |
| Monday | 5 years | 45 | Large room | 9.05 | Guitar | Head or class teacher |
| | 11 years | 65 | Hall | 9.05 | Piano | |
| Tuesday | 5–8 years | 270 | Hall | 9.05 | Piano | Head of Dept. |
| | 9–11 years | 205 | Hall | 9.25 | Radio | Deputy Head |
| Wednesday | 5–11 years | 475 | Hall | 10.10 | Guitar Recorders Percussion | Head or Deputy Head |
| Thursday | 6–11 years | 430 | Hall | 10.00 | Piano or improvised | Class of children |
| Friday | 6–10 years | 365 | Hall | 9.30 | Taped | Senior teacher |

In most schools there are opportunities to assemble in various formations - by year groups, houses and possibly even by sex. Such arrangements enable assemblies to be planned to accommodate a more homogenous group of people and might further enhance the occasions on which the whole school meets together. The programme can be made flexible enough to accommodate special occasions in the the school calendar, the beginning and end of terms, and those school weeks that mysteriously don't have five days in them.

Many people are still ultra-cautious about their assemblies. Yet many of these same people have made quite fundamental changes in their teaching methods in the last decade. Why then this lack of experimentation in forms of worship and assemblies in general? We need to make faith, and all that we do in this context, contemporary and relevant to the lives of children and teachers. To ignore the interests of most people in the group will remove that important element of relevance, the main catalyst for understanding. Since so many young children lack first-hand experience, and in some cases are not able to readily assimilate second-hand experience, we must deal with matters that they can be expected to understand. It is doubly important, therefore, to give them opportunities to shape the act. With very young children there will need to be a great deal of teacher guidance; at secondary level teacher consultation will be the practice.

For older children, and in this I would include 11-year-olds, assemblies have a special purpose. They can be thought of as a search for truth, and a quest for meaning and purpose in life. This can only be achieved by posing various questions and persuading young minds to think about the alternative answers. The various ideals, habits, duties and responsibilties of all people need to be made explicit. By examining the deeper aspects of the human situation, the child will come to know society's claim on him and, if the idea has appeal for him, God's. Obviously the degree to which each child can engage in this kind of exploration will depend upon his age, sophistication and the current attitude of society towards moral, social and religious matters. This type of assembly, if well done, will be a significant communal and personal experience and should be seen as an important element in the development of personality.

This advocacy of an open-ended approach does not mean any

lessening of the need for conviction and commitment, nor a watering down of Christian standards. No one should confuse the obvious tolerance shown among most faiths today with apathy. What is most desired is a new, or perhaps renewed, kind of response from those who allow the assembly tide to wash over them once a day, who will remain fairly untouched as long as they pull their limpet shell tightly down onto the rock-like chair or floor on which they are sitting. We are not after the reaction, 'What a lovely assembly', but rather 'That was interesting', 'That made me think', 'What am I going to do about that?', and so on.

# UP THE SCHOOL

Some head teachers would be rather surprised to hear children's responses to the question 'What did you hear about in assembly this morning?' I am thinking of one regular item that obviously imprints itself on young minds, and that is the state of their playground. The seriousness with which the head talks about the amount of litter around the school is crystal clear to all. What has gone before — some well-chosen reading from the Scriptures perhaps — is quite forgotten as the diatribe about sweet papers, sandwich bags and other miscellaneous materials continues. Children need occasional reminders of matters important to the running of the school, its general appearance and so on. If we raise these points with the assembled school before the problem situations reach serious proportions, we can discuss them without the venom that occasionally accompanies such infringements.

There are various ways of dealing with rules and requests, which should be kept to a minimum so that every child is able to remember them. It is of the utmost importance that children know why they must do certain things. The reasons usually concern the safety and welfare of the whole group, and the care of property. Perhaps you can devote one assembly to a discussion about the school and the democratic framework it needs for its successful operation. One assembly a week could be designated for dealing with all domestic matters arising in the school. It is important to know how the football team and the netball players fared in their last matches; that support is needed for the next production of the drama group; that woollens are needed in greater quantities if the school is ever going to get that mini-bus, and so on. Matters like punctuality could be brought up then too, but they might be used as part of another assembly — the beginning perhaps, and the idea developed during the meeting.

Some teachers object to a formal assembly being followed by a recital of sporting successes. I have sympathy with their views if they are in schools — not unknown — where an unsuccessful team or player is publicly pilloried. The inclusion of all and every kind of news will emphasise the assembly as an integral part of the school life. By interrelating work, play and worship in this way, the occasion will be seen as a time for the normal expression of the full vitality of the school.

The assembly is the outward expression of the community life of the school. Whether the assembly is religious or not, there is an enormous value in all the people in an organisation meeting together. The near-tribal feeling that is at its height when the full meeting takes place is not far removed from religion when, for instance, some joint concern is felt for the community in which the children live. This is why at least some of the assemblies should be secular in nature, so that attendance can be made compulsory and any divisive situations occasioned by religious differences can be avoided. The shared values of the school can be celebrated at the beginning and end of terms, prizedays, and on special anniversaries.

As well as an occasion when a sense of belonging to a community can be engendered, and as a platform for school ethics, assemblies are also valuable for the head teacher, and any other member of staff, in the creation and development of a relationship with the corporate body of the school. There are few similar situations in which this special kind of rapport can be achieved, and whoever is conducting the proceedings ought to take notice of this fact. Content and method need to be thought over with care as considerable as that given to any other matter in the curriculum.

The timing of assembly is also very important. There are strong arguments in favour of the assembly at the beginning of the day so that an orderly, thoughtful start can be achieved. The only problem here is, how early? If the bell goes at 8.55 a.m. and assembly begins at 9.00 a.m., one or two children will still be out in the cold! Someone may be detailed to field them as they creep into school, but if she has misunderstood her instructions, she might try to secrete them into the back row, where the pupils are having to strain very hard to hear and be attentive anyway.

Just before playtime is another popular time, but this places a severe strain on the organisation to make the event precisely fifteen minutes long on every occasion. To go on longer might incur the wrath of some staff members and the enthusiastic fourth-year footballers. Playtime can always be extended, but perhaps that would cut across the start of the 'Singing Together' broadcast at 11.00 a.m. Perhaps one might tape-record the broadcast, but what of the swimming session booked at the local baths? Is the end of the afternoon any more feasible or are some children in our classes, especially those in the inner city schools, too restless then to take part in a gathering of this kind?

Four o'clock is also very important to some people. I recall one teacher who made a brief nod to God with closing prayers each afternoon. Her routine, certainly for the winter months, was unchanging. She would demand that all the children stand, put their hands together and close their eyes. Then she would intone the prayer, each phrase accompanied by the donning of some article of clothing. First the hat, planted squarely on the head . . .

Hands together (left glove) . . . softly so (right glove),
Little eyes shut tight (scarf twirled skilfully around the neck),
Father just before we go (coat on with a flourish),
Hear our prayer tonight (buttons done up and belt fastened),
Amen (handbag picked up).
Eyes open, lead on.

Thankfully, few are like this, and the time of parting, especially for very young children, can be a most significant experience.

Find out what the children think about assemblies, and what changes they would like to see. You can do this by asking children informally in small groups in the playground, library, etc., or by circulating a questionnaire to a particular year group, to a sample throughout the school, or to the whole school.

Here is a typical questionnaire that can easily be adapted to suit the particular needs of the situation.

1  Do you like a daily assembly? If not, how often would you like to meet during the week for an assembly?
   At what time of the day do you prefer assembly?
   9.00 a.m.   10.00 a.m.   11.00 a.m.   11.45 a.m.   3.30 p.m.
   Other time
2  Do you prefer the whole school to gather together for assembly

or to meet in smaller groups?
For what purposes do you think the entire school should meet for assembly?

3 Do you like the assembly conducted by
one person          several people          children
teachers and children?

4 Do you like having visiting speakers in assembly?

5 Do you like to hear stories in assembly?
Does it matter what the source is? In other words, does it matter if the story comes from the Bible, a book, the newspaper, or someone's personal experience? Which form do you prefer?

6 What was yesterday's assembly about?

7 Mention an assembly that you remember as being very special.

8 After any assembly have you ever thought you would like to do something about the issue discussed?

9 Do you remember an assembly that helped you to understand something that had been worrying you?

10 Do you like to hear someone talking about something that has happened to them?

11 What do you remember about most of the assembly occasions you have attended?

12 Do you think attendance at assemblies should be voluntary? If so, would you come?

13 What do you think of radio assemblies?

14 What was the last one you heard?

15 Do you like to see part of an assembly dramatised?

16 What was the last dramatic assembly you saw?

17 Do you like to have films, slides, etc. used in assembly?

18 What kind of music do you like used in assemblies?

19 Do you know the name of the piece used today? Its composer? Who was playing it?

20 Do you like to come into the hall while music is playing, or do you prefer to sit and then have the music begin?

21 Which hymns do you prefer to sing at assembly?

22 What other songs do you enjoy singing at assembly?

23 Do you like prayers used during assembly?
Do you like to join in saying the prayers?
Do you like to listen to prayers that have been composed by your friends?

24 How do you manage with the language used in prayers and hymns?

25 What kind of assemblies do you prefer?

26 Would you be willing to help organise and run assemblies?

# A PLACE FOR ASSEMBLY

There are a few people — a very few — who, like Jesus, could keep
a gathering of thousands engrossed and involved on the side of a bare
mountain, oblivious to fatigue, hunger and discomfort. For the rest
of us, it is only realistic to consider the surroundings from the point
of view of comfort as well as aesthetics.

In order to promote the corporate identity it is desirable for
everyone in the school to meet together. Some schools do not have
a hall, and others do not have one big enough to accommodate
everyone. Closed-circuit television might be tried or radio relay
in a large comprehensive school. If the weather is suitable, perhaps
the assembly can move outdoors, using electrical amplification to
ensure that everyone can hear the speaker. There is a novelty and,
therefore, an appeal in such a change of venue. Similarly, you might
be able to use a hall in another building, for example, a neighbouring,
larger school or a church. In the latter case, one should inform
parents in advance so that they may have an opportunity of
objecting to their child attending such an assembly.

Frequently, especially at primary level, the assembly hall will
be the same space that is used for physical education, dining,
drama, music and movement work and other activities, and from
the clutter usually about one could identify all of the uses to
which it is put.

The assembly requires a particular setting, just as the P.E.
session or the creative drama lesson does. Most often you will want
to create a focal point. It can be positioned so that the drama blocks,
chairs and other equipment are out of sight, and so that the presenter
is at the front. He might have a low table with a bowl of flowers on
it, or a large assembly table with a small lectern on it, although this
does formalise the proceedings. Drama blocks could be arranged to
create a number of levels. Use drapes to break the sharp edges, and
provide a background for a display of relevant or interesting objects.
A stage setting of screens and drama blocks could be prepared for

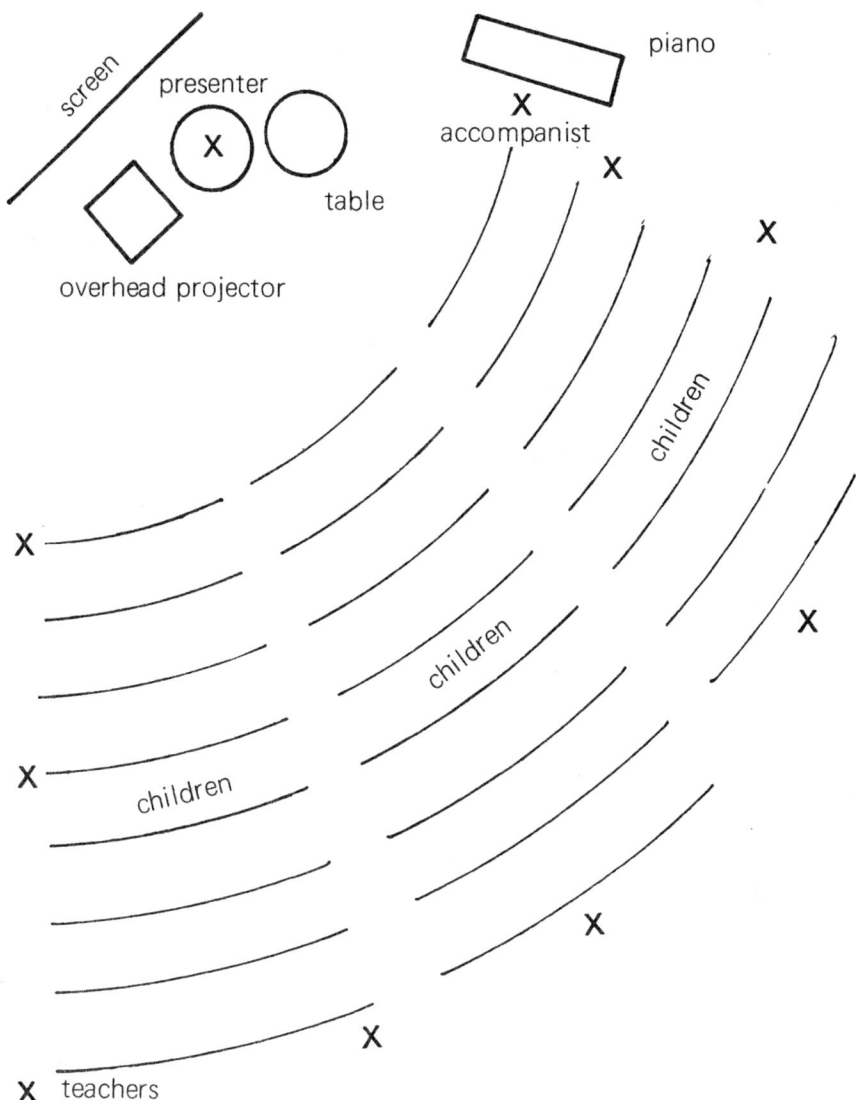

*A simple assembly arrangement*

a children's assembly. Some schools have a permanent arrangement of blocks in the middle of one hall and assembly is always carried out in the round.

The speaker, whether a child or an adult, needs to be seen when the audience is sitting or standing. A platform can raise a person into everyone's view, but it may also make him seem remote. Even a

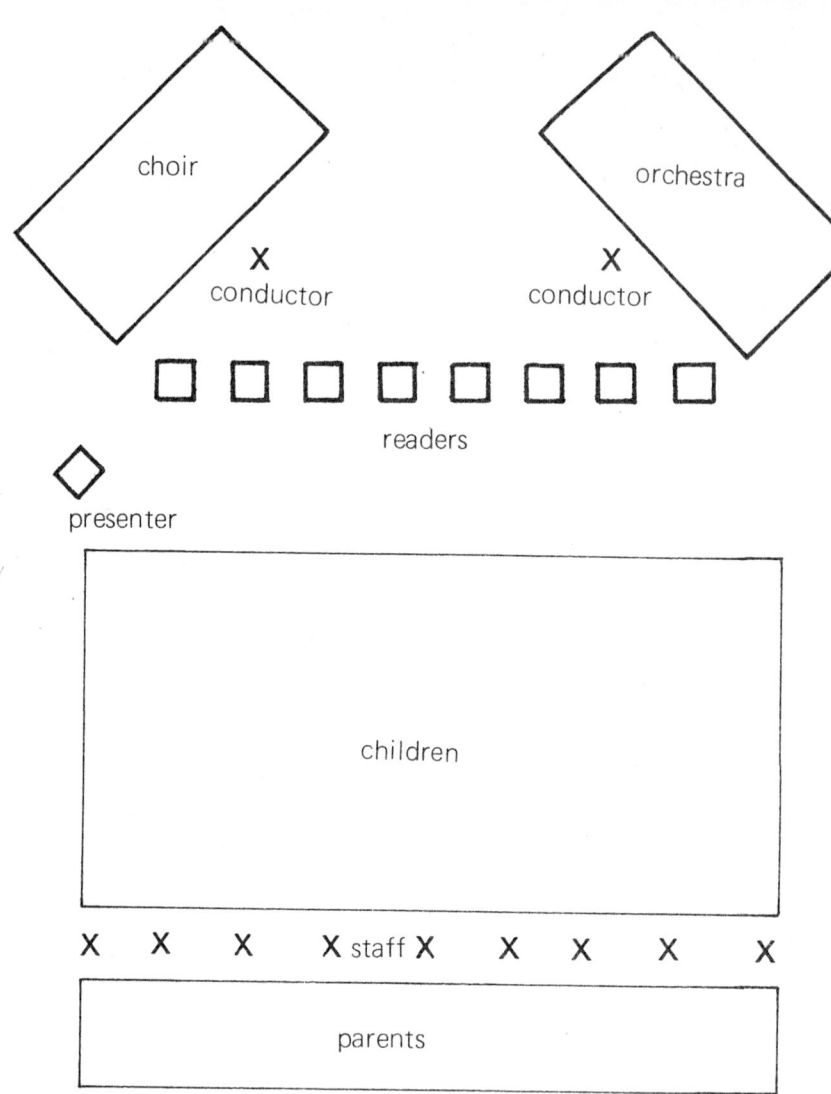

choir

orchestra

X
conductor

X
conductor

readers

presenter

children

X  X  X  X staff X  X  X  X  X

parents

*An arrangement for a festival assembly*

lectern or an assembly table can act as a barrier. Jesus resorted to a boat on at least one occasion, and spoke from the side of a hill to allow himself to be seen and heard by a multitude of people, but usually he would stand with the crowd around him. What he said gave him stature. You might prefer not to have any props, but just a small place that the presenter occupies, sitting on the floor among the children.

Chairs, small drama blocks or stools are usually arranged for
the staff at the back, along the sides, or informally around the hall.
At the age of 11 children suddenly appear to need chairs to sit on,
so at secondary school chairs for the pupils will be needed too.
Where space is at a premium, often the only solution is to carefully
line up every class across the hall, oldest at the back, youngest
and shortest at the front. Where space is not at such a premium, a
more informal seating arrangement can be suggested in which friends,
brothers and sisters can sit together irrespective of age or class. A
much more relaxed atmosphere accompanies such arrangements.
Teachers can deploy themselves around the hall in the same way.

Whatever furniture is required, it is important that it should be
ready before the first classes or groups begin to arrive. A well-
trained group of monitors, or children from a number of classes
in turn, can make an early appraisal of the needs of the particular
assembly and make the appropriate arrangements. Such preparatory
work can include draping materials, arranging flowers or displays,
moving equipment, finding hymn books and sheet music for the
accompanist, and organising records and tapes.

The presenter should be able to assess the temperature of the
hall before the service and decide how many and how much any
of the windows ought to be opened. Usually the hall will warm up
during the assembly because of the proximity of five hundred two-
legged radiators to each other. If this can be anticipated, it will be
so much the better for the atmosphere and any singing that might
occur. Quite a useful aide-memoire for the presenter to write at
the top of his notes is 'Heating, seating, ventilation, light', to ensure
that these factors are agreeable for the children and himself. Not all
adults will agree about the first and third points, but the presenter
should insist on his prior claims.

Phone calls, visitors and minor crises can occur at the most
inopportune times. However, in ordinary circumstances it is of
inestimable value to be ready for assembly five minutes before
time. By being in the assembly hall in advance of the children one
stands a better chance of feeling, if not quite serene, at least in a
good humour, welcoming and relaxed, and ready to lead a large
group of people in something worthy of the name of an assembly.

I have found nothing more unnerving than my arrival into a

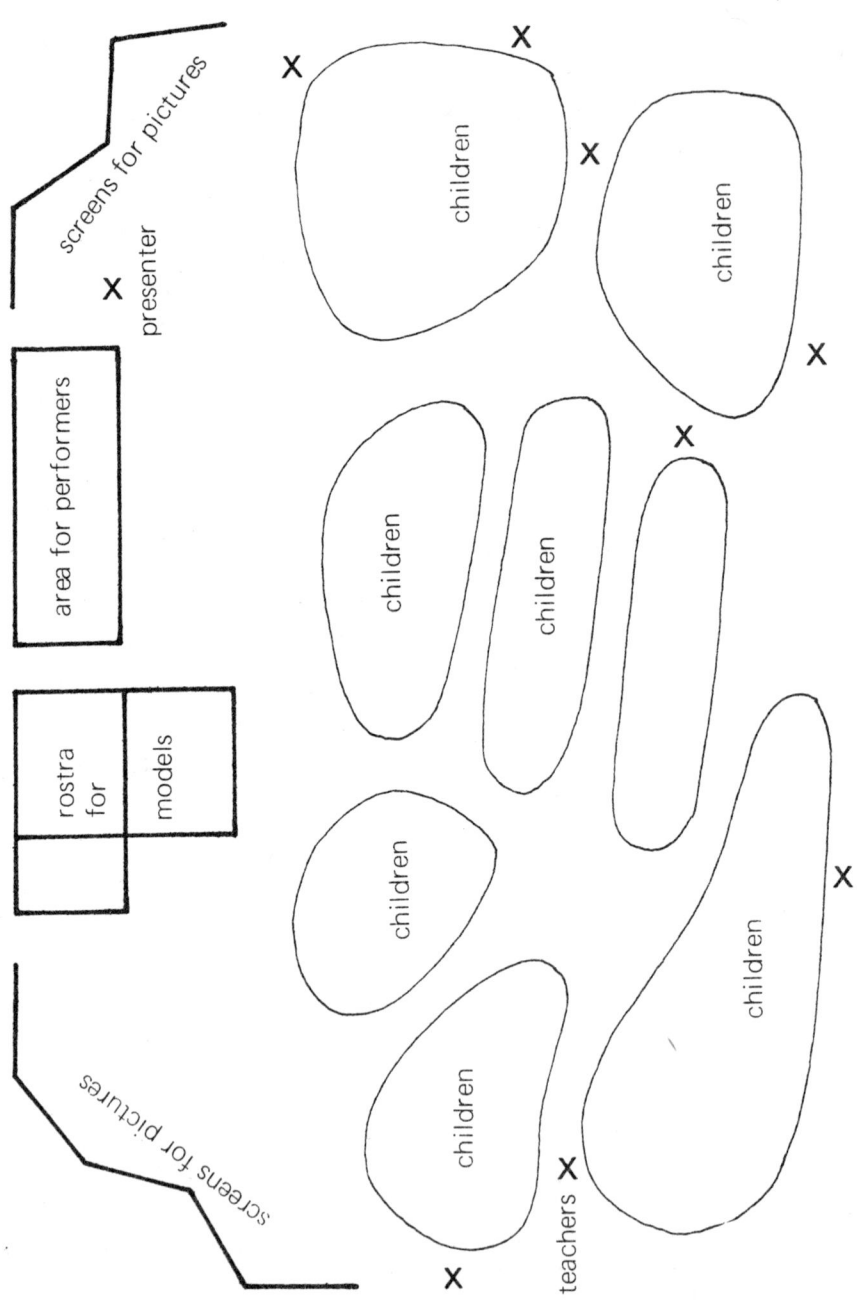

*An informal seating arrangement for an assembly on achievements*

hushed hall where the pupils had already assembled, and have had a distinct feeling of being like someone from outer space.

A bell can be used to summon children to the hall, but where a regular time is adopted (even varying from day to day) this should merely serve as a reminder. Alternatively, the hall monitors can quickly go to all the classes to say that the assembly hall is ready. If a loudspeaker system is available in the school, music can be relayed to each of the classes where the circuit has been left open. (See pages 124—127 for suggestions for music to use in assembly.)

If children have to come from another building or have just returned from an activity outside school, they should part with their outdoor clothes before the beginning of the assembly. The apparently surreptitious removal of a heavy overcoat in a sitting position is often of much more absorbing interest to other children than listening to the story of the Prodigal Son. Children will, in fact, see the act of removing an overcoat during an assembly as an activity to help pass the time.

An even more interesting diversion is the hurried sortie across the hall by a zealous teacher anxious to remove someone who is finding his smuggled comic of more consuming interest than the distant appeal to his moral sense. Usually the eagle eye of the teacher (obviously herself not too engrossed in the words of wisdom from the dais), or a word of warning passed down the line is enough to caution a child.

Do we in fact react too violently to inattention? Since we cannot really force attention of this kind on a young child, should we ignore what may only be a moment's departure? It is where the inattention of a few distracts the others that some sanctions need to be introduced. We might also bear in mind that the number of adults who fall asleep during a religious service is legion. Addison, in one of his essays on Sir Roger de Coverley, said that at church he...

> will suffer no body to sleep in it besides himself; for if by chance he has been surprised into a short nap at sermon, upon recovering out of it he stands up and looks about him and if he sees anybody else nodding, either wakes them himself, or sends his servants to them.

In spite of that lapse, anyone familiar with Sir Roger will know what a a shining example of a Christian he was.

# HANDS TOGETHER AND EYES SHUT TIGHT

Then Miss Watson she took me in the closet and prayed, but nothing came of it. She told me to pray everyday and whatever I asked for I would get it. But it warn't so. I tried it. Once I got a fish line, but no hooks. It wasn't any good without hooks. I tried for the hooks three or four times but somehow I couldn't make it work. I asked Miss Watson to try for me, but she said I was a fool. She never told me why, and I couldn't make it out no way.

So wrote Mark Twain, but how many children would agree with this?

Most children think of prayers as an indispensable part of the proceedings and when I first began to explore varieties of assemblies this was remarked upon frequently. Was it perhaps the only regular occasion in which they could participate — even if it was only by the act of closing hands and eyes together? When they are preparing their own assemblies, children will want to include this element. While the prayers are often related to the theme, the tendency to drift into the sentimental should be avoided.

Where used, the prayers should be within the mental grasp of the children and free from too many archaisms and the limited closed-circuit language of faith. All of this does not mean that prayers cannot be phrased in beautiful language. Choose short, simple prayers that are related to the theme of the assembly, so that everyone's thoughts can be brought together for a brief moment of maximum concentration. If the prayer that has been selected or prepared has a response, it should be a simple one to be repeated after each sentence. The sentences should be said slowly enough for them to be understood.

Some prayers are learnt, but if too frequently used are only repeated in a parrot-like fashion and produce interesting accidental and deliberate parodies. The Lord's Prayer has produced more of these than most prayers; for example, 'How father', 'Harold Be Thy Name', 'Lead Us Not Into Thames Station'.

A discussion about prayer with older children can be a fruitful activity. Is it any use? Should we act, rather than pray, about a problem? Perhaps the act of praying can so unite people that they may then see that they could act together. Once we have resolved to do something together, it is well on its way to being dealt with by united action. Certainly by thinking of prayer in this way we will be achieving the attentive response of the whole group and providing our proportion of energy and will.

There is always an answer to a prayer; in fact, there are four possible answers: yes, no, wait, if you do your part. Certainly a child should not consider that God is simply a switch to flick.

Prayer cannot interfere with natural laws. To pray for a fine day is fraught with problems. It is better to pray for a good time, whether it rains or shines; to pray that both teams might enjoy the game, rather than for a victory for the football team. It is no good asking in a prayer that we might escape some difficulty. To pray only under such circumstances would be to do so as a stranger. There was once a saint who was asked why he spent so long in prayer. He replied that he hoped that when he was desperate, his voice would be recognised.

What we need to seek is not escape from danger, but the strength to face our problems. It is little good asking God to make us good, if we are not determined to take positive action ourselves. One is reminded of Augustine's famous prayer: 'Make me pure, but not yet.' We need to be determined and sincere in our own wishes to do something about our condition if we intend to say prayers.

We can divide prayers into types — thanksgiving, penitence, intercession, and petition, although on occasions two or more aspects can be included. I recall one prayer composed and delivered in 1971 with some feeling:

> We thank you for decimal money. But we hope we will never have any more new money, ever, ever, ever, ever again.

It is sometimes interesting to read prayers written for specific occasions. What would children have to say about this prayer, composed over a century ago:

O Lord, thou knowest that I have nine houses in the city of London and likewise that I have lately purchased an estate in fee simple in the county of Essex. Lord, I beseech Thee to preserve the two counties of Essex and Middlesex from fires, and as I have a mortgage in Hertfordshire, I beg Thee likewise to have an eye of compassion on that county. And Lord, for the rest of the counties, Thou mayest deal with them as Thou art pleased. O Lord, enable the Bank to answer all their bills and make all my debtors good men.

That certainly could be described as a special kind of pleading.

There is a list of books of prayers and readings on pages 121—122.

# GOD IN THE DRAMA BOX — OR, HOLD ON, GOD, I'VE LOST MY PLACE

I have joined together two stories to make the title. How frequently one can take two or more ingredients from different recipes and produce one's own particular dish. It is one of the reasons why I hope that this book can be regarded as a book of ingredients rather than a collection of recipes.

The delightful story of Tobias was being enacted using the words of Tobit from the Apocrypha, David Kossof's version, and the play *Tobias and the Angel* by James Bridie (published by Constable). The boy in the class who had been cast in the name part was so disconcerted by having to take the lead and by the voice he kept hearing issuing from inside a drama block that he went home at 10.30 in the morning under the mistaken notion that it was lunchtime.

On another occasion, in another place, an earnest if forgetful child had to remind 'God' sitting behind the curtain (probably with his lines in front of him) that the conversation and action were going a little too quickly for her.

On a recent popularity poll in school the children's assembly came out a clear winner. Perhaps it was because it was by children for children. But it was also drama. At assemblies where drama is used, there is an extremely high level of concentration and memorisation of details.

In the last twenty or so years drama has moved, certainly in primary schools, from a position of an optional extra to that of an important (some would say essential) aspect of the educational programme. There is a book list on pages 111 for those who would like to study method and philosophy.

Drama probably owes its existence as an art form to religion. Through the performance of some ritual, possibly costumed, ancient man and his successors have faced the unknown, its mysteries and their fears concerning it. Scratch beneath the surface of many of our folk customs and you come face to face with devils and spirits, and the need to placate one and encourage the other. In medieval times the Miracle Plays were created, taking for their repertoire the stirring events in the Bible. The various trade guilds took over the responsibility for the production of these cycles of plays and would sometimes include aspects related to their own calling. One important aspect of these plays, of which we need to remind ourselves from time to time, was that the characters spoke in everyday language. Humour was also an important ingredient of such productions.

In the fifteenth and sixteenth centuries playwrights began to look to sources other than the Scriptures while still maintaining a highly moral and allegorical tone to their stories. The performance of one of these plays, for example *Mak the Shepherd* (from the Wakefield Cycle) or the *Fall of Lucifer,* as an example of the later style, is a rewarding activity.

The Mummers' plays are also ancient religious stories, which are frequently performed at Christmas time, on All Souls' Day, or at Easter in schools. *St George meets Bold Slasher* is an exciting play that represents the inner struggle of man.

Children's own ideas, with discreet advice from the teacher, can be used to present situations in a most dynamic way. Characters can be created from their imaginations; stories can be prepared that will help both performers and spectators to understand their own experiences. This re-examination of experience through drama is perhaps its most powerful influence. By taking part in such an enterprise the individual moves towards a fuller understanding of himself and others. Drama provides a unique form of cooperative contact, and a powerful creative opportunity.

Words are often inadequate to express our feelings and so we can explore the world of mime, dance and movement work to develop a form of non-verbal communication. The purists will tell us that the value is for the children taking the roles. To provide an audience changes what they are doing from child drama into something different. This view is accepted, but the audience should

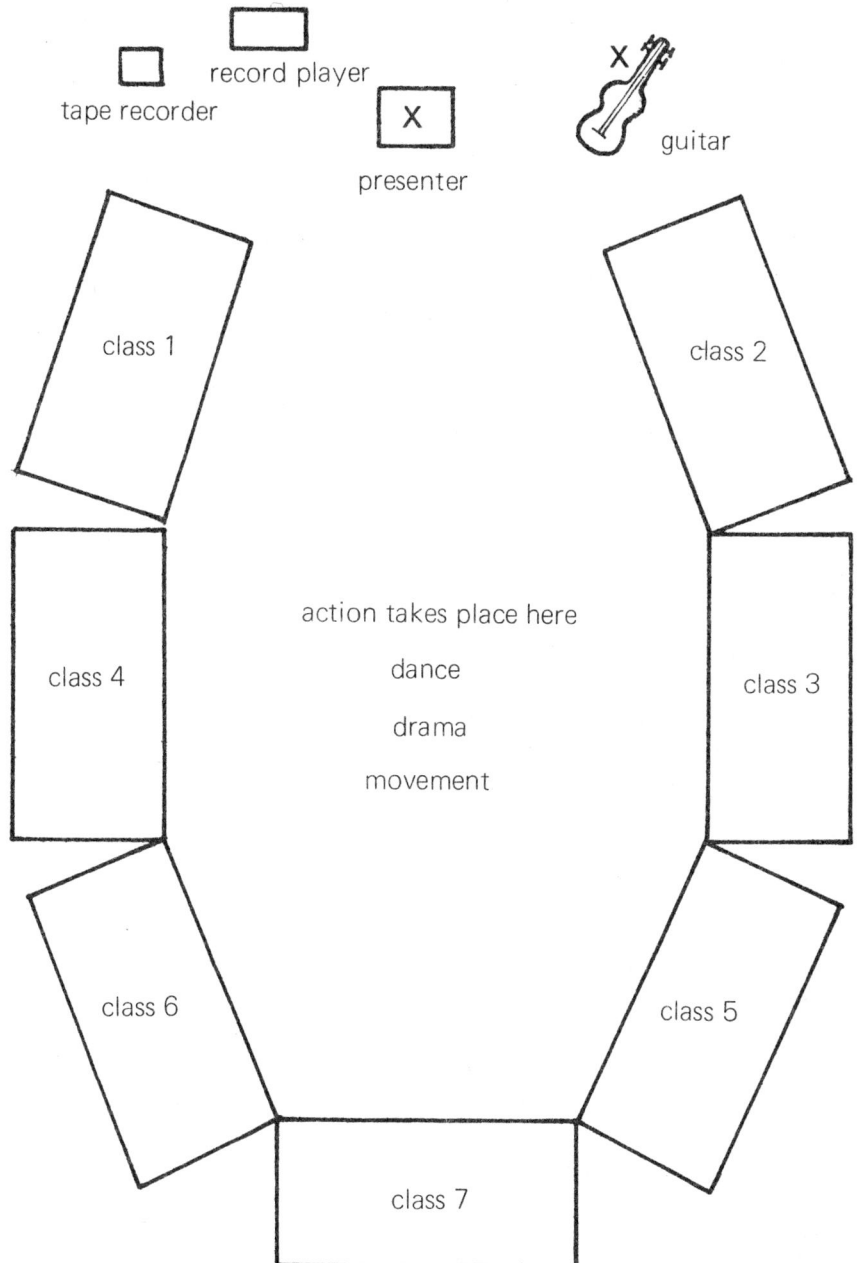

tape recorder

record player

presenter

guitar

class 1

class 2

action takes place here

dance

drama

movement

class 4

class 3

class 6

class 5

class 7

*An arrangement for an assembly in the round*

not be deprived of the opportunity of watching and learning from the conflicts they see portrayed in front of them.

The value of many such dramatic occasions will be heightened if the action and dialogue are presented in the round. Some of the most successful school assembly drama productions are those in which the audience feels part of the event. Children taking part can have their starting positions within the audience area. Entrances can be created in all kinds of places, and no more than two or three minutes work with chalk or masking tape can define these for classes arriving in the hall. Some schools cannot have theatre in the round because their stage is fixed. Perhaps they can build out an apron or provide additional acting areas elsewhere in the hall. The presence of a stage does go a long way to ensure that everyone is at least seen during the play. Where drama blocks are not used throughout, or the performers sit or lie down during the action, the audience becomes fidgety and inattentive.

Once a term is about sufficient for each class to contribute an assembly. The preparation for it, if it is going to be done satisfactorily, is very time consuming. Frequently the class can take the opportunity to describe some aspect of the work that is engaging their attention at the time, providing a progress report as it were. Very often within any thematic study there are elements that in some way illuminate man and his relations with others. If the school has a particular interest in an event of local, national or international importance, whether religious or otherwise, the class might be invited to use it as the theme of their assembly.

So often the quality of what is done is dependent on the skill and experience of the teacher, rather than the age group of the children concerned. Teachers in their first year can be invited to present their children's programmes after having seen the work of other classes. If they are lacking in confidence, they should be able to consult colleagues. They may, however, be happier to ask their children to present an assembly in a way that differs from the other assemblies, which because it is different will have just as much impact.

It is important to convince everyone that they are not contributing to a drama festival in which there is adjudication or comparison. While it is hoped that due attention will be given to

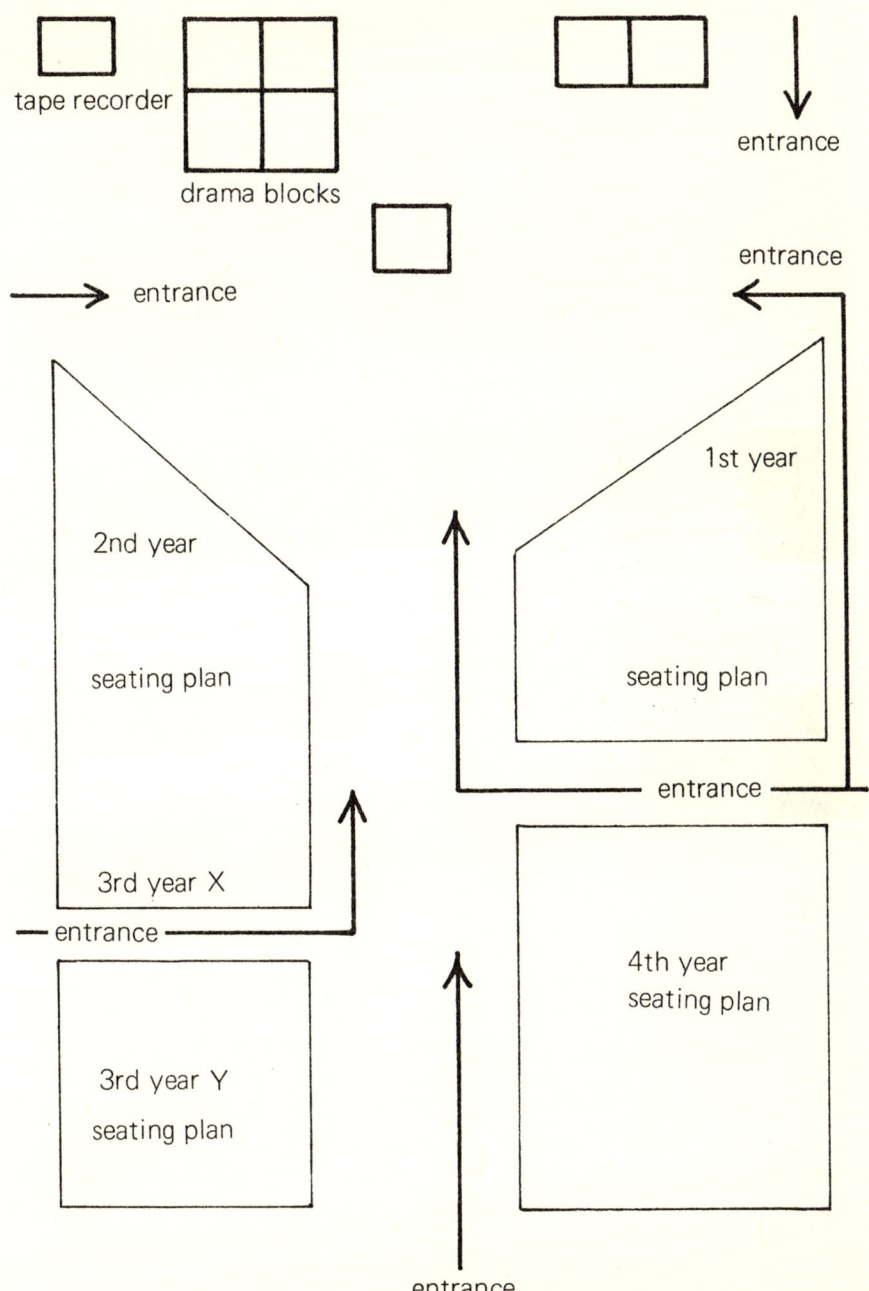

tape recorder

drama blocks

entrance

entrance

entrance

2nd year

seating plan

3rd year X

entrance

1st year

seating plan

entrance

3rd year Y

seating plan

4th year
seating plan

entrance

*An arrangement for a dramatic assembly*

the preparation of an assembly, it is important that it is not over-rehearsed, so that an inordinate amount of time is given to it, possibly denying others the use of the hall or taking time from other pursuits. The criteria ought to be the success the class has in being heard, seen and understood.

I recall being in one school where there was a moratorium declared on children's assemblies because each one appeared to have little more intention than to be better in some way than the previous one. By the end of the term, some of the productions, for indeed that is what they were, ended up as Hollywood spectaculars; perhaps this is what happened to religion in some places.

I take it upon myself in my school to voice the appreciation for the children's assemblies. This includes highlighting a significant point, or recalling for attention a smaller item,, possibly a remark made by one of the children, so that we can think more deeply about it. This kind of summary, or underlining, is particularly important where one or more characters is inaudible at the back of the hall. (In some schools the noise from the kitchen is dominant in the hall. A monitor can be alerted to stick a notice of 'Assembly in progress' on the back of the kitchen door, or perhaps the cook and kitchen staff might be invited to share the occasion.) I recall one class presentation of John Steinbeck's story *The Pearl* that was so moving that further words would have been superfluous or even diminished the impact. I felt that we had all been spectators at a very powerful drama. From such occasions as this, one might hope that the mature child will re-examine areas of his own experience and develop an awareness of others.

The choice of material is a matter for careful consideration. As already mentioned, the class and teacher can decide to focus attention on work they are doing or on an experience they have had. They have already, one assumes, been stimulated and so discussion about the form should proceed fairly quickly. Junior children need only a small amount of stimulus to bring to life ideas they have been discussing. The teacher should exercise control over the form of the story during rehearsal. Introduce the story, discuss it and allow individuals to express their ideas, link fragmentary episodes, and work out ways of disciplining violent action (if it is absolutely necessary to include it). Once the children have been placed in situations evoking speech and thought, their grasp of their roles will be more confident. With the most modest of props and the children's developed power of suggestion and confidence, the hall will be transformed into a fresh location.

The child is by no means an extension of the teacher, but the teacher needs to assist in the development of the story, for little more than chaos can result from completely free improvisation.

We must beware of extravagant claims about the effect of such dramatic experience on later actions. The child cannot forget the element of pretend in the situation. However, by being placed in a problematical situation children will be undergoing a kind of rehearsal for the future. The children in the audience should, through watching, listening and feeling, be stimulated to think about various forms of human experience and how people react to them. For young children it is enough to have a story to tell in action. For older pupils an open-ended situation is better. If this is done with conviction, sincerity and understanding, we will be able to claim that at least the children have discovered more than they knew before the experiment started.

Sometimes an audience inhibits the performers. Within the normal drama period situations can be evolved that would, by my definition, be called assemblies, and from them comes a very deep understanding of the human condition. To give a very obvious example, for the children to close their eyes and grope their way around the room trying to recognise objects, would give an insight into the world of the blind person, be it Bartimaeus or Helen Keller. Then to be met by Jesus or Anne Sullivan would make them think about consideration and compassion, and ways in which we might alleviate the suffering of our fellow man.

Child drama is essentially doing rather than showing. While the work probably has in a sense been rehearsed, new movement and conversation may be introduced so that even 'on the day' it might possibly be a new creation. It is important that the class and teacher have agreed on what is being illustrated, so that any new feature will vitalise and enhance the performance.

The judgement of any such children's offering should not be made by adult theatre standards. Afterwards it is valuable to discuss with the group the content of their programme and invite them to say which aspects had the impact that they had hoped, and which did not and why. Children are quite sensitive to atmosphere, not just the obvious situation when someone drops something unintentionally, but the subtler occasions when there is a falling off of attention if a monologue is too long, or the action has slowed down.

On page 119 there is a list of drama books.

# THE PLACE OF STORIES IN ASSEMBLIES

To meet the needs of teachers taking assemblies, there is a
great deal of help available from books (see pages 110–111). Some of
these books contain illustrative stories that carry a strong message.
Many of them might be regarded as modern parables, and as such
are invaluable. Jesus knew the value of this kind of vehicle. The
Bible abounds with examples that still have great point today.
There is a Hebrew parable that illustrates this argument
successfully.

> Truth walked among men naked, but received no welcome – some
> mocked him, others turned away in shame. One day, walking sadly
> along the road, he met Parable looking gay in his multi-coloured
> robe and asked him,
> 'Why is it that men avoid me? Am I old and ugly?'
> 'No,' laughed Parable! 'Take some of my clothes and see what
> happens.'
> Truth did this and found himself welcome wherever he travelled.
> Men cannot face the naked truth. They must meet him disguised in
> some way.

An examination of the Biblical parables indicates clearly the use
that Jesus made of homely illustration. Many of these stories can be
updated. For instance, he chose some of his stories about the farmer
and the fisherman because he and his audience either followed these
occupations or were near neighbours to them. Perhaps we need to
look for our stories in the factories and the urban situation.

Readers of the penultimate pages of women's magazines are well
aware that there are only a limited number of situations and they
tend to go on repeating themselves with only minor variations as
though they had never happened before. The same is true of all
human stories. We must provide the mantle that will give the story
a new freshness. How disappointed the new disciples were when they
gathered around John to ask for some truth to carry to the people.
'Tell the people this – children, love ye one another.' They protested

that they had told the people this before. But John insisted that now and always this was the Saviour's true message. But there is a need to look, like the disciples, for different ways to say it, otherwise our audience will not be held.

I am quite sure of the powerful quality of the well-told apposite story. Even the most able advocate will use an anecdote by way of illustration. Some would argue that the message will be understood by all who are able to comprehend. But there can be little wrong with preparing the 'stage' a little, providing some thought-provoking statement that is then expanded through a story. At the end, a question or two, possibly rhetorical, might move someone to seize upon one of the meanings within the story.

Great care must be exercised in any attempt, however, not to point out in too much detail what the story 'means'. How frequently one has seen this situation on the television epilogue when we are treated to a closeup of the speaker. The anecdote is delivered; we are gripped; then the smile leaves the face, the voice becomes unnatural and a chill descends on the proceedings; we are in church and gloom envelops us. This kind of solemnity, which one associates with dying, will evaporate much of the attention that has been built up. The story therefore needs to be a simple one. Where a large age range is present the choice of tale needs to be one that will interest the younger element. The older children will enjoy the experience nonetheless. With some stories they may appreciate certain subtleties that escape the attention of their younger brothers and sisters.

Where the story has been taken from a particular source, it is useful to credit it, for even this might make some particular impact. In the preparation of the assembly programme one needs to be familiar with the story and develop ways of making it one's own. Unless the language is particularly beautiful, or one is using someone's actual conversation or address, it is usually better to tell the story than to read it. If in the planning stage the story is modified, altered slightly to make it more immediate, expanded so that the salient points have digesting periods between them, so much the better.

The apocryphal tale is told of his lordship in Stepney giving advice to his young curate on how to improve his sermons. He told the young man how he used a personal anecdote to enliven his message. The curate took the advice literally and when he spoke from the pulpit on the following Sunday, he told the same story — unfortunately he prefaced it by saying 'When I was the Bishop of Stepney . . . . '

I find it helpful to write down the story or key points from it. I take time to look at this memory aid just before the assembly and during the delivery if there are some features, an unusual name, for instance, or a catalogue of names, that I need to see again. One does not want to slip up by transposing names or by forgetting to mention some important aspect of the story.

Where the story is a myth, legend, or fairy tale, introduce it by saying so. It is foolish to pretend a literal truth in a situation that could not happen.

> Two hunters were surprised by a huge bear. Both ran away hoping to reach a refuge. One reached a tree and climbed it, but his friend tripped over a root. He lay quite still and the bear approached him, snuffling around his head. Appearing to think the man dead, the bear ambled away. When it appeared safe to do so, the man descended from the tree, and ran towards his companion on the ground. Seeing his comrade well, he tried to be lighthearted about the situation. 'The bear seemed to be talking to you. What did he say?' he asked. Rather shaken and upset, the other hunter, thinking he would say what he thought, replied, 'He said that I shouldn't place too much faith in a friend who deserts me when things become difficult.'

In telling that story I would make it abundantly clear that the man who lay still on the ground pretended that the bear had spoken to him.

Where I can, and there are very few situations where this would be impossible, I would introduce some objects on which the attention could be focused. These need to be large enough to be seen and recognised by everyone. The overhead projector is useful too, in that transparencies can be prepared to illuminate the story. These can be opaque objects, such as animal silhouettes (see Can I Bring a Friend?), or they can be drawn with the appropriate pens. One can prepare a series of overlays around a single transparency so that the picture is built up as the story proceeds. Another interesting way to approach the telling of a story involving a journey is to prepare a background scene on the acetate roll and underneath it fix a transparency on which the main characters are drawn. As the roll is moved across the overhead projector, the figures appear to be moving. A map can be prepared on the roll, and a ship, aeroplane or other form of transport can be drawn on a sheet of acetate. With another pair of hands to help, all kinds of manoeuvres can be demonstrated. Such a presentation needs to be prepared, and a decision made upon its value in getting over the story and its message. Elaboration without careful planning, over-confidence in the machines and one's ability to manipulate them can lead to disaster.

Children can be invited to take part in the story. It is often a good idea to speak to one or two children when they are assembling and ask whether they will feel like joining in. Usually one knows one's children well enough to know which ones are likely to react in: the right way, and sometimes they will provide some impromptu action or dialogue that one can use to advantage.

One needs to be a collector of tales. There are numerous books that contain large numbers of them (see pages 118—119). Like any anthology, one will be immediately attracted to some stories more than others. I have found a number of my favourite books on second-hand bookstalls. The books are long out of print, but they contain material I can use or adapt. I copy down stories from all kinds of places. If you write them on cards you can arrange them in thematic groups. I look not just for any good story, but for one that will illustrate the point I want to make. I know which tales I have used with particular groups of children and I try not to repeat myself too often.

A school that is alive and developing is bound to build up its own folklore and a fund of well-loved stories. By repeating a few such stories, we underline the unity we hope exists in all our schools, and which has expression in our assemblies.

As well as making others' stories our own, there are situations that might be turned into stories. Jesus was a most inventive raconteur. He had a compassionate insight into the human situation. By observing the behaviour we see around us, it may be possible to develop that kind of insight. We might also note how Jesus turned back most of the questions so that those searching for truth could discover the answer themselves. When we are truly aware of our condition, revealed to us by this technique, we may well be able to do something about it.

# A FUNNY THING HAPPENED TO ME
# LAST WEEKEND

In an informal chat with a number of children I asked what kind of assemblies they enjoyed most of all. They responded that they liked those assemblies in which I talked about what had happened to me during the previous weekend.

Things happen to everyone; you see incidents, hear stories, cause things to happen, all very personal and real. From most of these situations it is possible to extract something for other people to to consider. We might regard some people as 'situation-prone' because everything seems to happen to them. Quite frequently they also happen to be good raconteurs. Pehaps they embellish a story to make it more dramatic, embroider a descriptive detail to add interest and give the listeners time to become engaged, or marry two or more incidents into a continuous narrative. But stripped of all the additives, the basic story needs to be a true one to fall into this category.

Such incidents can often stand in their own right as the central part of an address. On other occasions they might be a contemporary illustration to be used alongside a Biblical incident or to support some philosophical idea. What one needs to decide is whether or not it is necessary to draw a moral, or if it is more valuable for the children to be invited to consider then and there what they had learnt from the story.

I do not rely on the chance of something coming my way that I can use in assembly, but I have on a few occasions abandoned my plans because just such a situation has arisen.

For 'last weekend' in the title of this chapter, one might read any time in the past. I have used stories of things that happened to me when I was a child, when I was on holiday in various places; stories about people I have met and things I have found. I might occasionally make a number of apparently unrelated points that gradually, as the assembly proceeds, link up into a story.

Possibly to anticipate a comment, most of the situations that can
be used are really quite ordinary events and all that one is doing is
revealing the familiar and commonplace, something that is there
for all to see.

I once asked a friend of mine who always seems to have a vast
fund of stories whether she ever wrote them down. She said she
didn't because there really was no shortage of ideas; to travel on
a bus, wait to be served in a shop, to keep her eyes open was all that
was required. I tend to write down ideas myself — what I have seen
or been involved in. I usually use them within a short time, but
occasionally will find that they don't lose their value by being
kept several years.

# NOW TURN TO HYMN NUMBER ...

A school needs music. It needs to experiment with music.
Most assemblies, though not all, would be impoverished without
music in one form or another. Traditionally, the children's
participation in assembly music has been limited to singing one
or two hymns of Victorian vintage, the volume and sweetness of
sound depending largely on the dynamism of the head or music
teacher and, to a lesser degree, on the length of that sometimes
iniquitous weekly practice. Some teachers regard hymn practice
as an opportunity to have a staff meeting, do some marking, or
have a respite from their toil. Surely its main function should be
to increase the repertoire, raise the quality of the singing and, above
all, ensure full participation and enjoyment.

Some people would argue that we ought to omit all gloomy and
sentimental hymns. If we then cull those that are incomprehensible
and eliminate those that seem to demand a direct profession of
faith, what would be left? Should we perhaps include some of
these types of hymns just in case the children decide to go to
church?

Whatever we decide to sing, we need to look at the words to
see how theologically loaded the material is or what misleading
impressions might be handed on. Perhaps we could go through the
words of some of the favourite hymns and do a little rewriting,
altering a phrase here and updating an archaic word there.

If the children have any literary experience, they can also
participate in writing refrains, hymns or songs. They can, for
example, select and arrange the words to support a particular
theme. These songs can take a valued place in the regular
assembly singing. To write completely new words to known
and popular tunes can also give a topical and local flavour to
a situation.

At an infant assembly it is important that the children participate in the singing. If the choice of material is appropriate, the children will be able to join in at least some of the songs. Often the change of only one word in a line produces a new verse. *Kumbaya* is perhaps the best-known example of this, and is understandably popular. *Mary had a baby* is another song with minimal changes between verses.

Modern tunes have been written to accompany many old hymns. Because the tunes are vigorous and contemporary they appeal to the children of today as, no doubt, the originals did to those who sang them a century ago. Folk music also has a large part to play, and for about a decade we have had varied and imaginative material to offer young people to sing.

The natural instrument to accompany these modern hymns and songs is the guitar. Many schools enjoy the presence of at least one accomplished performer on this instrument. The guitar makes a refreshing change from the piano, which in some hands has a debilitating effect on the singing. Unaccompanied singing is an attractive variation from time to time, as is music on recorders or more sophisticated instruments.

It is important to be continually enlarging the repertoire because after a while *Kumbaya* and *The Lord of the Dance* can become stale. Lists of collections of hymns and folk songs are on pages 122–123. You can keep this list up to date by examining any new material that is issued. A list of records is on pages 124–126. Recorders are useful for teaching new items and providing a different accompaniment, as well as an opportunity to play. Listening to someone who can sing well helps the children to learn the song. Where the music is particularly tuneful and the words easily understood, there is little to prevent them learning a new song quite rapidly.

If a teacher has the necessary confidence and the ability to sing or accompany, it is a good idea to introduce a new song during an assembly. When the words are simple, perhaps repetitive, instant singing can produce a great feeling of pleasurable achievement.

The children can hum to a tune, clap hands, or even whistle. Whoever is conducting the assembly will have to decide whether to risk the whistling. Anyone experienced in working with groups of children is usually aware of how far they can be allowed to go.

If accompanists are in short supply, prepare a special tape on which at least the most popular material is recorded. You can make additions to the tape from time to time. It is a good idea to have the title, number, or first line of the song announced on the tape. A fairly generous space should be left between each item so that the hymn can be found quickly and accurately. Normally, whoever is conducting the assembly will have already located the item and checked the volume level. But where a second piece is required, the counter numbers may not be precise enough to locate the announcement on the tape, and it is a little disconcerting to be hunting for the first verse of *Onward Christian Soldiers* and find yourself in the middle of *Oft in danger, oft in woe.* Similarly, the arrival of the last verse may find one napping. The race across the hall to the tape recorder or the signal to the duty operator might be a bit delayed, and one would find oneself launched on another item that might be inappropriate to the theme being developed.

The choir, on the day the visiting accompanist comes to the school, might find the creation of a taped hymnal a satisfying challenge, and be able to provide a considerable selection of music over a number of recording sessions. It is always a good idea to ask them to sing the first verse as an introduction, and then repeat it, assuming that everyone will join in on the reprise. If the routine is established, the children will know what to do each time.

Where only musical accompaniment is provided, the player needs to watch the timing very carefully. The pace should be consistent throughout the hymn, and slow enough for young children to keep up with. This is not to suggest that a selection of dirges is required – a tempo fractionally slower than usual will probably be sufficient.

Whatever the hymn book chosen, the collection is never quite as complete as one would like. The thought of children carrying two or more books is rather daunting. These books are frequently in short supply and poor condition. The hymn book is often the most used book in the child's possession and he may gradually shred it to pieces, especially if what he is subjected to is dull and prolonged.

46

Some schools arrange their own anthologies in a looseleaf folder, to which additions and deletions can easily be made. Many other schools use the modern equivalent of the suspended hymn sheets, preparing transparencies of the material required and using an overhead projector to produce an image large enough for everyone to see. The transparencies can be written on inexpensive pieces of transparency. Binding all four edges with tape makes the transparencies quite durable. They can be filed in looseleaf folders, one corresponding to each of the many accompanist's books the school can afford now that it doesn't have to replace fifty tattered hymn books a year.

Mounts are slightly more expensive than the folders, and are probably a better investment in the long run. Where transparencies are used in the teaching of hymns, parts of the verse can be marked to focus attention on a particular line or word. Children are quite capable of operating this and most other machines, thus releasing the teacher to concentrate on other aspects of the occasion.

Song-making is a bit like learning to swim. After the first hesitancy, one takes the plunge and progress is slow but sure. Often one can use a well-known tune as the basis for a new hymn.

Here are a few examples of home-made material. The first song was used as a link between items in an assembly. The words were taken from the Bible and were God's promise after the Flood. There are four lines to be sung.

While the earth remaineth seed time and harvest shall not cease
While the earth remaineth summer and winter shall not cease
While the earth remaineth cold and heat shall not cease
While the earth remaineth night and day shall not cease

The following song came from Tidemill Infants School in Deptford. They sing it to the tune *John Brown's Body*. The first line of each verse and the chorus are sung three times; the chorus is sung after every verse.

47

1 The stalls of Deptford Market are all filled at
   Christmas time,
   As we walk home at night.

*Chorus:*
   Praise the Lord for all his goodness,
   As we walk home at night.

2 We will save up all our pennies and we'll buy a gift for you,
   As we walk home at night.

3 We will wrap up all our presents and we'll hide them all away,
   As we walk home at night.

4 We will sing and dance at parties so we hope that you'll be
   there,
   As we walk home at night.

5 We will laugh and pull the crackers and we'll eat the party fare,
   As we walk home at night.

6 We will sing our thanks to Jesus for the gifts for us to share,
   As we walk home at night.

I next met the children the following autumn and they had adapted
the words to:

   The stalls in Deptford Market are all filled at harvest time, etc.

They also had interesting verses about their environment with first
lines such as,

   The dustmen bang their dustbins in the corporation cart;
   The totter from the Arches trots along behind his horse;
   Our mothers do their shopping and buy food for me and you.

Another school used the Parable of the Sower as the basis for a
very exciting dance drama. Mary Hutton of Adamsrill School had
worked with the children to produce a song that acted as the
opening and closing feature of the assembly. Try clapping the
rhythm of the lines below and note how they scan. A guitar player
would have little difficulty choosing chords to develop a tune to

fit the metre. The first line of each verse and the chorus are sung three times; the chorus is sung after every verse.

1 A sower went out to sow the seeds,
   And they fell all over the ground.

*Chorus:*
   Sow the seeds in the good ground
   And the seed is the word of the Lord.

2 Some of the seed fell on the path,
   The seeds were trodden down flat.

3 Some of the seed fell on thin soil,
   And the birds ate it all up.

4 Some of the seed fell on rocky ground,
   So it withered away in the sun.

5 Some of the seed fell on bad ground,
   But the thistles choked it to death.

6 Some of the seed fell on good soil,
   So it grew and it was good corn.

Music can be used in assemblies to create an atmosphere, as support material for another kind of programme, or as the central theme. Whatever its purpose, music for assemblies should be chosen carefully. The length of the piece to be played and the number of occasions when it is to be used require careful consideration. Well-chosen music can have a calming effect on a group of children. Only if the atmosphere is right can we expect children to respond to an assembly presentation. As a rule, avoid music in which there are abrupt changes of volume, rhythm or harmony. One of my colleagues once complained that the assembly music I had chosen, *A Walk in the Black Forest,* had had disastrous effects on her congregation.

Your school may be fortunate enough to have a member of staff particularly well-informed about music, able to select appropriate pieces, and enthusiastic to share his knowledge with the children. The children need to know what the music is called, who composed it, by whom it is played and on what instruments. They should be given the opportunity to suggest answers to these questions, especially the latter one. Children who receive a well-balanced musical education will, over the years, become interested and knowledgeable. Children can be asked to indicate their reactions to pieces of music. Certainly in this field everyone is entitled to his opinion.

When a descriptive piece of music is used, the teacher who chose it can be invited to spend about five minutes discussing the background details of the composition.

When music is tape-recorded, particular sections can be found easily, and fading in and out can be achieved. Finding the correct track on a long-playing record is not easy, the presentation of one's back to the children inappropriate, and the scratching of a record that might accompany the removal of the playing head can completely ruin the atmosphere built up by the music.

It is very refreshing to include live music in an assembly. Perhaps your school has an orchestra, or band, or talented soloists among the children or the staff. You might also want to invite musical groups from neighbouring schools to perform at one of your assemblies (see page 76).

Here are some of the compositions we have used in assemblies in recent years.
*Pictures at an Exhibition,* Modeste Petrovich Mussorgsky
(quite the most popular because of the treatment of it picture by picture and the follow up in artwork by the children.)
*Hary Janos,* Zoltan Kodaly.

The next three pieces were selected and introduced with very short extracts prior to school performances of the story.
*Lieutenant Kije,* Serge Prokofiev
*Petrouchka,* Igor Stravinsky
*West Side Story,* Leonard Bernstein

These three portraits can, with wit and ingenuity, be used as the central part of a series of assemblies.
*Peter and the Wolf,* Serge Prokofiev
*Till Eulenspiegel,* Richard Strauss
*The Sorcerer's Apprentice,* Paul Dukas

50

Here are just two of the many pieces that can be used for the beauty of the melody.

*Concerto for Piccolo,* Antonio Vivaldi
*Appalachian Spring,* Aaron Copland

Here are a few examples of music that can be used to herald a religious festival, or set the scene for a particular type of assembly.

*The Four Seasons,* Antonio Vivaldi
*The Pastoral Symphony,* Ludwig van Beethoven
*The Messiah,* George Frederick Handel

The following selections were played during a term to show how different composers have expressed their impressions of the sea in all its moods.

*La Mer,* Claude Debussy
*Sea Songs,* Benjamin Britten
*Hebrides Overture,* Felix Mendelsohn
*Scheherazade,* Nicholas Rimsky-Korsakov

The *Classical Symphony* by Serge Prokofiev was adopted to introduce a regular school broadcasting about books. It was given a few airings before being used as a signature tune.

The 'Orb and Sceptre' movement from *Crown Imperial,* by William Walton, was used for several weeks to prepare the school for a festival celebrating the nine hundreth anniversary of Westminster Abbey, and to the children's forthcoming visit to the Abbey.

The *Young Person's Guide to the Orchestra,* by Benjamin Britten, was used for some weeks before the school was shown the film featuring it, *Instruments of the Orchestra* (Central Office of Information). In addition, records that featured instruments in groups or solo were played. With the help of the local comprehensive school, many of the instruments were shown to the children and played.

# SO YOU THINK YOU'VE GOT A GOOD ASSEMBLY?

I think we all know many a good assembly that has taken place without all the soul and heart searching and labouring that I ask you to engage in. Such assemblies have been conducted by people who weren't the sort to have analysed all that they were doing — or were they? Perhaps they did employ this analytical and synthesizing approach subconsciously.

What is the time of the assembly?
What do I hope to achieve by using this theme for an assembly?
Is it a topical theme?
Is it for a special occasion?
Has it international, national, or local significance?
Is the theme within the children's experience?
Is it within the children's understanding?
How will I present it to suit the age range of the children?
Is the theme one of a series of assemblies?
What kind of approach will I make in presenting this theme?
What are the alternatives?
Will the adopted course be something quite new for the children?
If so, how will I ensure that it succeeds?
How can I involve the children?
    Listening; singing; engaging in discussion; playing music; performing
    a play; demonstrating; puppetry; dancing; other ways.
How can I involve the staff?
Have any of the staff or children had any related experience that
could be used?
Would it be helpful to invite a guest speaker?
What kind of music do I need for the assembly?
What other resources do I need for the assembly?
Are they available in the school? Where else can I get them?
Do I need to make a display of pictures or other materials?
What kind of background information do I need to gather to make
the assembly a success?
Is there anything that some or all of the children can do after the
assembly, immediately or in the short term?

Possibly this approach will encourage us to take a very critical look at our assemblies. It may be helpful therefore to have a further checklist for use in the assembly hall to ensure that nothing has been forgotten.

No doubt the best and most appropriate music has been chosen, and the story to be told, the drama to be acted out, or the programme to be presented has been prepared. Is the organisation the best that can be provided? It would be a pity if it were not since so much work has already been done.

During the last war I underwent flying training, and on graduating to twin-engined aircraft I was suprised by the complexity of the cockpit on first seeing the Anson aeroplane. But all was well because I was provided with a pre-flight checklist. There must have been more than fifty items on it that had to be ticked off after a drill. It ensured that one got off the ground safely. So why not a checklist for assemblies? If this idea appeals, then the book could be opened at this page until the drill becomes second nature.
On occasions it might, by jogging the memory about a particular item, remind you to include an aspect that had been overlooked. In many cases only a few sections will be checked off. But in others, festivals or other special occasions, you may need a considerable amount of organisation and the checklist will probably ensure a little less stress beforehand and a more relaxed assembly.

## ASSEMBLY CHECKLIST

**Setting**

Person responsible:                              Notes:

Day:                        Time:               Duration:

No. of children:                                Age range:

Theme:

Assembly area to be used:

Arrangement of children:

Seating for presenter:      staff:
  visiting speaker:     visitors:

Decoration:

Table:    Rostrum:     Drama blocks:

Ventilation:         Lighting:

**Contributors**

Staff:

Children:

Visitors:

**Music**

Introductory and closing:     Record:

Illustrative:         Tape:

Interlude:          Live:

Player or T/R:  speed  needle  record  volume
  warm-up time    operator  track or counter number

Choice of song, hymn or other music for participation:

Music for:  accompanist  choir  orchestra  soloists

Instrument for accompanist:  piano (unlock)  guitar
  other

Words and music to be learnt:

Words for children:  books  duplicate sheets  hymn sheets
  O.H.P. transparencies  slides  other

Instruments for children:

## Readings and displays

Books to be read from:          On display:

Children's writings to be read from:      On display:

Pictures:          Friezes:          Posters:

Models:          Objects:

Display:

Blackboard:          Flannelgraph:      Magnetic board:

Whiteboard:          Teaselboard:

## Audio-visual aids

O.H.P. projector: positioned      focused      screen
   O.H.P. transparencies   pens   other OHP aids

Slide projector:   positioned      focused      screen
   slides ordered and correctly positioned

Filmstrip projector:   positioned      focused      screen
   filmstrip loaded      checked

Tape recorder:   positioned      checked      track      speed
   tape

   Synchronization checked with slide or strip where appropriate:

Radio:      check station      time      volume

Film projector:   check position      focus      speed      sound
   screen      film loaded      checked      rewound

TV:      network      video tape      position      warm-up
   channel      contrast      volume

   Video tape loaded      checked      rewound

For all audio-visual aids
    Operator:
    Method of cuing:
    Sufficient electrical points:                    Adaptors:
    Extension leads (check positions):
    Person responsible for hall lights:
    Spare bulb available:                   Spare fuses available:

For some visual aids blackout will be necessary. When and by whom will this be done? (Some can be done before the assembly to avoid distraction.)

Projected aids:                    best position for screen
    maximum size picture in relation to light

**Drama productions**

Rehearsal:

Narrator:

Costumes:                    Props:                    Scenery:

Drama blocks (monitors to position and reposition):

Entrances:

Sufficient space:

Sound effects:              tapes:          live:

Readings:                  tapes:          live:

Music:                     tapes:          live:

Puppetry:    puppets    stage    dialogue    tape    live

Other items special or peculiar to your building, children, philosophy or approach.

See pages 112—113 for books about audio-visual aids.

# Part 2

# INTRODUCTION

I am conscious of the fact that there is always too much to
do and that some people reading this book, possibly only glancing
at it, are wanting instant assemblies. I hope that they can make
time to read Part I, and possibly agree that assemblies are important,
that an enormous amount of social, moral and religious value can
accrue from carefully planned occasions, and, therefore, that
imagination and effort given towards their preparation is worthwhile.
I would like to reiterate that this is a book about assemblies rather
than exclusively about religious worship. I have avoided any kind
of protracted ecclesiastical ritual or tendency to deal with morals
like tables, to be dealt with one by one.

Children of all ages expect and need a certain amount of routine.
However, what they do not need is what must seem to them to be
the identical assembly everyday. The alternative is not to present
a bewildering series of happenings in which the pupils feel insecure.
Changes need to be made gradually. The introduction of anything
new should not be in the spirit of 'Well, that was quite interesting,
but we will have an ordinary assembly tomorrow.' Any new item
should be included because it brings variety to the scene and because
it is as good, if not better, than some other approaches.

Everything we do must relate directly to contemporary life,
otherwise children will quickly spot the irrelevancy. By this, I
don't necessarily mean that we have to adopt the vicar-on-the-
motorbike approach or feel that without a guitar in our lap we
will not command attention.

What we do in assembly must be a matter of individual conviction.
The approach will be directly affected by the beliefs of the teacher,
and his ability to handle particular situations. Most of us have
experienced occasions when particular people have electrified
us, and we happily admitted that we would never be able to do
the same kind of thing or get the same standard of work out of
children. But we can sometimes modify or adapt what other people

have done and, after some experience, achieve a satisfactory result.

We may also find that a particular new approach is not for us, but others in or out of the school could be invited to conduct an assembly in this way so that the experience of the corporate body of the school is widened.

It might be suggested that we are in danger of turning our assembly hall into a three-ring circus, or that the elaborate arrangements we are making are going beyond the measures necessary to interest the children and are merely entertaining them. If the variety of aids and the type of presentation are so elaborate that the message is lost, then there is no justification for their use. But in other cases, slides, overhead projector transparencies, film, recorded sound and music are now such familiar resources elsewhere in the school that to ignore their possible use in assemblies would seem rather puritanical. They can be useful in extending experience, but as with any aid used in teaching, relevance of the material and the opportunity to preview are vital to their successful use.

This book is not intended as a pattern book, but a kind of assembly sampler in which a number of ideas are explored. It is really a help you to help yourself book. No anthology suits everyone and readers are invited to select from the lists of assembly books on page 110 for other ideas. Particular hymns, songs, or music will need to be chosen to fit the programme that is being built up. Occasionally, where some music or other aspect is particularly relevant, has universal appeal or may not be generally known, suggestions have been made. Similarly, if prayers are to be included, it is best for the teacher to find one from one of the books suggested on page 122 or to compose one with the children.

# TODAY IT IS WINTER

The changing pattern of the seasons is a feature that can be
introduced into the recurring cycle of assembly themes. The
idea can be extended to include all the variations of the weather.
There was once a group of parishioners who looked forward to
the vicar's weekly prayer of thanks for mercies received. After
suffering a week of quite appalling weather, with torrential rain
from Monday to Sunday, they sat dripping and waiting in their
pews. Their vicar did not disappoint them. 'Thank God,' he said,
'it is not always as bad as this.'

An interesting programme about winter could be developed
using some of the materials below. Apart from the films, which have
to be booked in advance, it would be possible to prepare the
programme well in advance and keep the material in cold storage
until an appropriately wintry day. The assembly could then be on
the theme 'Today it is winter'.

## BACKGROUND INFORMATION
Why we have seasons
How the seasons affect plant and animal, including human, life

## PRESENTATION
Music:  Vivaldi, *The Four Seasons,* the 'Winter' movement
Display of winter material collected by children and presenter
Pictures of winter that are large enough for everyone to see:
silhouetted trees, winter feeding of livestock, tracks in the snow, etc.

Poems and readings about winter: a group of children or teachers
to read their favourite pieces about the season. The readers can be
arranged on chairs or drama blocks. They should be familiar with
the material and be able to recite it or read it smoothly.

## POEMS

Blake, William: *To Winter*
Bridges, Robert: *London Snow*
Clare, John: *Sheep in Winter*
Davies, W. H.: *Winter's Beauty*
De la Mare, Walter: *The Snowflake*
Frost, Robert: *Stopping By Woods On a Snowy Evening*
Shakespeare: *When Icicles Hang by The Wall*

## FILMS

*Animals in Winter* (Encyclopedia Britannica)
*Snow* (National Film Board of Canada)
*Snow* (British Transport Films)
*Snowflakes* (Moody Institute of Science, USA, and British Film Institute)
*Children in Winter* (Rank Films)

## SUPPORT MATERIALS

Natural materials
Pictures by the children in which only black and white have been used.
Silhouettes
Patterns of snowflakes
Collection of winter transparencies from different years
Collection of winter pictures from old issues of colour supplements, *Amateur Photographer*, BBC and IBA broadcast pamphlets
Stories about winter written by the children

## DEVELOPMENTS

Excursions inspired by the assembly; for example, into local parks, woodlands, and countryside to collect material for display.

Excursions to other relevant places of interest, such as the Polar Room of the National Maritime Museum, the *H.M.S. Discovery*, moored on the Thames Embankment. Such visits would provide opportunities for classes to report back to the assembly on the theme of winter.

Development of a winter festival. See 'Winter' in *A Book of Festivals* (Mills and Boon).

## THEMES FOR SIMILAR TREATMENT

Use all the seasons for at least one year so that the annual cycle is fully explored.

Devise a series of short assemblies that explore the way the seasons affect animals, people and plants. This requires a good deal of preparation, and the careful selection of material to provide short assemblies.

The elements, earth, air, water, and fire, would make another series that could be richly illustrated.

The assembly could be built around a particular occasion, such as a spring flower show. The bulbs the children had planted the previous autumn would make a good display. Usually there are one or two staff members who, with a team of children, can create a delightful display. See a 'Festival of Flowers' in *A Book of Celebrations* (Mills and Boon). Similarly, a summer event can be arranged after the children have grown seeds at home or in school.

An outdoor assembly could be held after planting trees in the grounds of the school (in wooden or concrete pots if your school has no gardens).

Have a harvest festival, perhaps with a different emphasis than usual, concentrating on the work of the farmer, on food, famine, production of food abroad, and so on.

# JOSEPH

The Bible is the most valuable source of story material. The ILEA
Agreed Syllabus of Religious Education refers to the Bible as a
quarry, and we can seek there the precious ore we need.

The story of Joseph is one from which we can gain all kinds of
insight into the human condition. As well as being a story of
incident, excitement, intrigue and success, it is episodic and so
naturally lends itself to serial treatment. Providing that the story is
well-presented on each occasion, there will be a tremendous feeling
of anticipation at each assembly when the next part of the story
is told. The major device of the serial story — the cliff-hanger — can
be used with great effect. When the time comes for the next
instalment, a short recapitulation will be necessary. By asking
the children appropriate questions you can get them to supply
the recapitulation themselves. In one part of the story I asked
why Benjamin had been dragged back to Joseph. One child
answered, 'He had nicked the silver.' That child had certainly got
the detail of the story, and from the style of his reply I could tell
that he thought the action quite justified, even though a little
trickery had been involved.

Combining the gifts of researcher and story teller, David Kossoff
has taken many of the Bible stories and retold them on radio,
television and in print. The Joseph story, for example, is told
about every two years as a serial on the programme 'A religious
service for primary schools'. The great advantage of David Kossoff's
material is that it is very easy to use. Therein lies the danger that the
school will be treated to an exclusive diet of the David Kossoff
version of the Bible. Through overexposure the work may fall
into disrepute in the children's eyes. I always like to read the Bible
telling alongside the Kossoff version, or any other version that I find.

## BACKGROUND INFORMATION
The history of Joseph, Genesis 38-45 (-50 for the remainder of
his life)

De la Mare, Walter: *The Story of Joseph* (Faber)

Diamond, L.: *The Story of Joseph* (Ladybird Books)

Kossoff, David: *Five to Ten* Second Series (BBC)
     *Bible Stories* (Collins)

Waddell, H.: *Stories from Holy Writ* (Constable)


## PRESENTATION

Serialisation as a straight narrative. Episodes:

1 The jealous brothers
2 The quarrel
3 Joseph goes to Egypt
4 Potiphar's wife
5 Joseph and the dreams
6 The famine
7 Joseph meets his brothers again
8 The family reunited

Dramatisation: Create a large number of parts, with crowd scenes at the slave market, in prison, in court, etc.

Music and movement: The story can also be interpreted as a dance drama, with music composed by the children or carefully selected to suit the particular episodes. Recently the Bible has become a rich source of ideas for the composer and lyricist. One very successful venture has been *Joseph and the Amazing Technicolour Dreamcoat* by Andrew Lloyd-Webber and Tim Rice (piano score from Novello and Co.).

Slides: Where a dramatic presentation has been prepared, and costumes and props have been assembled, take a series of slides to use in the recapitulation, or to put in the school's resource material file for use at a later date for a different kind of presentation.

## SUPPORT MATERIALS

Costumes, props and backcloths for dramatic presentations

Series of models showing episodes from the story; a class could be invited to produce a model each week to illustrate the story as it develops. Simple figures made from pipe-cleaners or dolly clothes pegs with colourful material stuck into position can form the basis for each scene. Where space is at a premium, low-relief models can be made in a series of similar cardboard boxes.

A giant figure of Joseph might be attempted to signify his domination in the story. A large wooden armature would be needed for legs, backbone, shoulders, pelvis and arms. Use chicken wire to fill out the torso, arms and legs, and to mould the head shape. Use papier mâché to cover the framework of the head, forearms, hands and feet. A long, beautiful coat can be made from paper or cloth to cover the rest of the body.

## DEVELOPMENTS
Discussions on family life and forgiveness

## STORIES FOR SIMILAR TREATMENT
Samson
David
Jacob and Esau
Gideon
Joshua
Ruth
Samuel
Jonah
Tobias
Moses
Adam and Eve
Cain and Abel
Daniel
The conversion and journeys of Paul
Pilgrim's Progress - with a great deal of help from the relevant section of *Thieves and Angels* by David Holbrook (Cambridge University Press) and *Every Child's Pilgrim's Progress* by Derek McCulloch (Epworth Press). When we used this story, the last episode was recapitulated by a drama group using flannelgraph technique before the next one was told. An overhead projector would be an even more effective aid. One might prepare a background on an acetate roll and overlay transparencies with characters drawn in.

# ALWAYS IN THE WRONG

A wolf spied a lamb drinking from a river, and wanted to find some pretext for eating it. Accordingly, he stood upstream of the lamb and accused it of spoiling the water. The lamb protested that it was only drinking with the end of its tongue, and besides it was downstream of the wolf.

'Anyway, last year you insulted my father,' complained the wolf.

'But I wasn't born last year,' answered the lamb.

'You are rather too good at finding answers,' said the wolf, 'but I'm going to eat you anyway.'

Moral: When someone is determined to do you down, he will refuse to listen to any reply, however justified.

So runs just one of the many fables that provide interesting material for assembly themes. The most familiar fables are those accredited to Aesop, writing in the fifth century. Most of the stories are about animals that have adventures and frequently speak and behave like human beings. They provide convenient vehicles for teaching particular moral lessons since people seem more receptive to criticism and advice if it is directed towards animals rather than themselves.

## BACKGROUND INFORMATION

*Fables of Aesop* (Penguin)

De la Fontaine, Jean: (seventeenth century French writer): *Fables* (Harrap) (in French)

Tolstoy, Alexei: *Russian Tales for Children* (Routledge and Kegan Paul)

Andersen, Hans Christian: *The Ugly Duckling* (Child's Play); this story is especially suitable when it is linked directly with Andersen's life story. The assembly could be rounded off with a recording of Danny Kaye singing the song *The Ugly Duckling* from the film *Hans Christian Andersen.*

Rudyard Kipling's *Just So* stories might be used in this context.

Androcles and the Lion, and Chaucer's *Nun's Priest's Tale* could be useful stories in a similar vein.

## PRESENTATION

Simple reading or telling of story

Dual presentation: one person miming the story and the other expounding on the moral and drawing the lesson from the children.

Present the story or a series of fables with the use of animal puppets or masked characters.

In some of the fables, group response may be possible from the audience. For example, when the monkey, after dancing, is elected king by the other animals, the vote can be elicited from the audience; or the audience might be asked whether the donkey ought to venture into the lion's den the second time, and so on.

## SUPPORT MATERIALS

Puppets of characters in the fables
Animal masks for use in dramatic presentations

Background music, e.g. Charles Camille Saint-Saens' *Carnival of the Animals*

Poetry: There is a vast range to choose from in various anthologies; particularly *Four Feet and Two*, compiled by Leila Berg (Penguin), *The Penguin Book of Animal Verse*, compiled by George Macbeth (Penguin). See the poetry anthology list on page 121—122 for others.

Invite the children to write a fable to present at assembly. Where French is a regular second language, the record *La Fontaine's Fables* (Everest FRL 152) could be used with some free translation from French by the children or teacher afterwards.

Here is a fable written by a child about Britain's entry into the Common Market. Readers will probably see much more in the story than the simple moral given by the author, but that is what is so remarkable about stories.

### Two Dogs and a Bone

There was once an English bulldog called Charles and a French poodle called Michelle, and this story happens in England. When two dogs met they found a bone and neither could decide who had seen the bone first, and they both wanted it.

'I say, which one of us should have it?' said Charles.

'Me, of course,' said Michelle.

But the bulldog was hungry as well as the poodle, so they decided to fight about it and the winner would get the bone.

While they were fighting a tiny little dachshund from Germany called Fritz trotted along, picked up the bone, and then ran off with it. The two dogs stopped fighting and Michelle said 'Sacre bleu,' which is French, and Charles in a typically English voice said 'I say, it didn't do us any good by fighting did it?'

Moral: You never achieve what you want by fighting for it.

Sharon Williams (10 years)

# IT'S THAT MAN AGAIN

I asked one child why he didn't seem to like assemblies. He replied
that they were always about 'that man'. Having experienced the
conditioned response of children in an assembly or religious
education class, who answer 'Jesus' whatever the question, I assumed
that the child was referrring to him. However, on being pressed
further, he revealed that he was tired of hearing about none other
than the Good Samaritan.

It is certainly a well-known story and, possibly because of its
simplicity, has held men's minds since Jesus told it as a parable.
The danger of the over-exposure of such stories is obviously a very
real one. Perhaps we need to keep a record of the themes explored
in assemblies. I say 'explored' deliberately, because such is the
power of this story that it can be dealt with in a variety of ways.

## BACKGROUND INFORMATION
Luke 10: 25—37

## PRESENTATION
A reading of the story from the New English Bible

A reading of the story as told by Bernard Miles; 'A Kindly Gipsy'
from *God's Brainwave* (Hodder and Stoughton). You can also play
the record of Bernard Miles reading this story, and others, in his
best Hertfordshire accent: *God's Brainwave* (Decca ACL 324).
There is another telling of the story by Carl Burke in *God Is
for Real, Man* (Collins), in which the Samaritan is called 'a real
cool square' and 'band-aids' are applied before a lift is given in a car.
I'm sure that with the transatlantic interchange of television
programmes the children will find no difficulty with the
message.

Prepare a series of transparencies showing the various characters
in the story. On the acetate roll provide a background of the town,
then the countryside with rocks and bushes and, further along the

road, a wayside inn. Rotate the roll on the overhead projector and introduce the other figures on the transparencies. Alternatively, use silhouettes of the figures as the scene is unrolled. Have the story told by children.

## SUPPORT MATERIALS
Folk songs: *Jericho Road* (in *Folk Sound* - Galliard)
*When I Needed A Neighbour* (in *Faith, Folk and Clarity* - Galliard)

Tape-recorded sounds: busy town scene, footsteps, conversation of villains waiting in ambush, the attack, groans, footsteps approaching and receding, horse and Samaritan stop, etc.

A fabric collage with all the events and characters portrayed.

## DEVELOPMENTS
After telling the story invite the children to see if they can think of any extenuating circumstances for the apparent disregard of the wounded man by the other passers-by. These are some of the reasons second year junior children at St Joseph's School in Deptford thought the characters might give

| | |
|---|---|
| The Priest: | I can't believe my eyes. It looks very suspicious. It's probably a trick — someone might ambush me. |
| Levite: | Perhaps he's one of the gang. He's only pretending he's dying. |
| | I'm terrified at the sight of blood. |
| | Somebody might say that I had done it — they might convict me. |
| | I'm too busy. I have got to see the king — I must not disobey. |
| | Somebody else will come along and help him. |

Here is what they said about the motives of the Samaritan.

| | |
|---|---|
| Samaritan: | If I don't help that man, I'll feel guilty all my life — I could never forgive myself. |
| | When I go to heaven it would be a mortal sin if I did not help him. |

Prepare a group poem of the story. The one below was written by Class 5, Hitherfield School in south-west London.

71

Dusty, stony,
Twisting, dangerous
Was the road the traveller took,
From Jerusalem to Jericho
He was alone.
All of a sudden he fell among thieves
Who whipped him and stripped him
And left him to die.
Along came a priest.
Nothing did he do.
Along came a Levite
Who stared, but passed by.
Then came a Samaritan
No friend of a Jew.
His heart full of pity
He bound the man's wounds.
He took him to an inn
Money did he pay.
There the Jew recovered
And went on his way
Grateful.

Present the poem as choral speech, or set it to music and sing it.

Write as a modern version of the story. Present it as a play.

Discuss: problems of poverty, thugs, differences of race, colour
and creed preventing people helping one another.
What to do in emergencies.
What is a neighbour? (See 'A Festival of Good Neighbours' in *A
Book of Celebrations*, Mills and Boon.) Ask the children what they
understand by a neighbour. Here is a selection of responses from
a class of 8-year-olds at Boxgrove School.

He is someone who helps you in your troubles.
Someone who comes to see you on your birthday.
Someone you can trust. Someone to share things with.
Someone who helps you when you have nowhere to live.
Someone who looks after you when you are ill.
Someone who fights your battles with you.
Someone who helps you when you are in difficulties.
Someone to play with.

See *One in a thousand,* a poem by Rudyard Kipling.

## STORIES FOR SIMILAR TREATMENT

Jesus used many parables. Some are better-known than others because of their significance to individuals and society today, and because the ethics they express are largely common to all great world religions and so very easily comprehended.

Prodigal son  Luke 15: 11—32
The sower  Mark 4: 1—8; Matthew 13: 1—8; Luke 8: 4—8
The lost coin  Luke 15: 8—10
The lost sheep  Luke 15: 3—7
The labourers in the vineyard  Matthew 20: 1—16
The grand supper  Luke 14: 15—24
The king's feast  Matthew 22: 1—14
The unforgiving debtor  Matthew 18: 23—35
The hidden treasure  Matthew 13: 44—46
The wicked winedressers  Mark 12: 1—11; Matthew 21: 33—43;
Luke 20: 9—18
The rich fool  Luke 12: 16—20
The bailiff  Luke 16: 1—8
The Pharisee and the tax gatherer Luke 18: 9—14
The two sons  Matthew 21: 28—32
The magistrate and the widow Luke 18: 1—8
The five foolish maidens  Matthew 25: 1—13
The talents  Matthew 25: 14—30

I would like to close this section with a quotation from the Bible:

> In all this teaching to the crowds Jesus spoke in parables; in fact he never spoke to them without a parable; thus making good the prophecy of Isaiah: 'I will open my mouth in parables; I will utter things kept secret since the world was made.'
>
> (Matthew 13: 34 and 35)

Immediately afterwards the disciples in private asked him to explain the parable of the darnel in the field . . . and he did. Later still, having found out that they understood now, he said, 'When, therefore, a teacher of the law has become a learner in the kingdom of Heaven, he is like a householder who can produce from his store both the new and the old' — which is also food for thought.

# AND WHAT WOULD YOU LIKE TO SHOW US?

The act of sharing is fundamental to the idea of assembly, and
a regular opportunity can be taken in school to extend this concept
to include the displaying of work and talent.

## BACKGROUND INFORMATION
The work of a particular class or pieces of work in the same
subject, say music or writing, from each class can be used. This
might even be limited to a single theme, for example, writing about
animals or going on a journey.

## PRESENTATION
It is important for the person conducting the assembly to know
what is being offered. If it is something to see, then it must be
big enough to be seen by the people at the back of the hall. If
the group is a small one, this may not be a problem; but where the
gathering is large, the model or picture must be large too.

Where the work to be shared is a piece of writing done by a
child, it must be audible to everyone in the hall. If this is a first
appearance for the writer, he should have a chance to rehearse.
It might be necessary for someone else to read the work rather
than have it inaudible.

Musical items, whether they are first efforts on the recorder or
a complete orchestral piece, should also be carefully rehearsed, so
that the audience is treated to a performance, not a chaotic
cacophony.

When you have gathered the material, you may find that you have
too much and must make a selection. Save the other material for
future assemblies. Where a theme has emerged or has been used to
stimulate the contributions, you need to decide on the order of
presentation. Pace, variety and climax are the main considerations,
but the 'nerves' of a particular participant (or her teacher) might
determine her place in the programme or position on the stage.

A linking commentary, which might be read by one of the children, should be short and clear.

Drama blocks might be used to raise speakers or performers to a level where they can be clearly seen. Screens could be erected so that pictures and other visual aids can be pinned in position rather than be held, usually not quite straight and slowly sinking like the setting sun. If an element of surprise is necessary, a sheet of paper can be pinned over the picture for later unveiling.

## SUPPORT MATERIALS

The class or group of children concerned might like to choose appropriate music to be used during their programme. It might be on record or tape, or be an original composition. They can choose songs or hymns to be used during the assembly, which might include a chorus they have composed that can be quickly learnt by the other children in the school.

OHP transparencies might be used for new song material or to provide illustrations. The overhead projector is a versatile machine; it can be used to show such things as magnetic fields, insects in closed transparent containers, wave motion, and so on. Consult books on the OHP for other suggestions on how to use it (see page 113).

If the class has made 35mm slides or an 8mm movie film, the correct equipment will need collecting and arranging in the hall before the school assembles.

## DEVELOPMENTS

After the assembly it should be possible for the children to examine the material that has been shown. Perhaps it can be left on display or be put on exhibition elsewhere in the school — the library, the foyer, or a corridor. Alternatively, it can be taken around the classes for closer examination.

The particular theme may have been chosen deliberately to stimulate further work elsewhere in the school, or perhaps the imagination displayed in the idea will stimulate interesting work for individuals, classes, or even the whole school. The visual impact of the assembly might stir members of staff who had not been inspired by a staff room discussion. The follow-up ideas could serve as assembly ideas for later weeks in the term.

## THEMES FOR SIMILAR TREATMENT

As well as the work on show from different parts of the school, invitations can be extended to neighbouring schools to display their work or special talents. A secondary school with a West Indian steel band might be pleased to have their stars invited to perform at the local primary school.

It is important that we praise hard work and effort, and to do so in public will pay large dividends. Children who have displayed a special talent or made excellent progress during the term might well have a spot in an appropriate assembly. Staff members could be invited to display their talents too, singing, playing an instrument, demonstrating a craft, or reading a favourite piece.

One 'and what would you like to show us' assembly at Boxgrove School during the Christmas period includes these items in the programme for the upper school:

> second year children displayed and wore masks they had made, and performed new agility exercises they had learned;

> third year children showed and talked about models and paintings they had done;

> fourth year children demonstrated their needlework skill, and played accordions and recorders.

The assembly was introduced by the playing of the record *Little Drummer Boy*, and a parallel was drawn with the children of the school sharing their talents with each other.

# THIS WEEK I WOULD LIKE YOU TO MEET THE POSTMAN

Some children seem to know more about the Eskimo and the Pigmy than they do about their own countrymen. Where relevance is a factor in deciding curriculum content, studies of the environment local to the school are sure to feature regularly in the programme. Everyone in the school can benefit from visits by people who serve the community in different ways. Invite such people to join in a series of assemblies so that the contribution they make to the community can be explored.

The postman, a very familiar figure to everyone, is a good choice to begin the series. He may be a parent of a child in school, which means that he should have some idea of how to communicate with young children. If a particular postman is requested, for example, the one who delivers in the area or to the school, it might be necessary to alter the time of the assembly to fit in with his work schedule. Make sure that he comes in uniform, as this will have special appeal for the younger children in the audience.

## BACKGROUND INFORMATION

Anticipate the visit by a display of relevant books from the library. Perhaps a particular class is doing a project on this week's guest and have 'cornered' all the reference books. They might be persuaded to allow at least some of the books to be available in the corridor or hall display the day before and after the postman's visit.

Here is a short booklist:
Adams, H.: *Postmen and the Post Office* (Blackwell)
Briant, F. Heathcote: *The Postman* (Ward Lock)
Ford, Tony: *Postman (Choosing A Job)* (Wayland Publishers)
Page, R.: *The Story of the Post* (Black)
Southgate, V.: *The Postman and the Postal Service* (Ladybird Books)
Sealey, Leonard: *Using Your Post Office; Letter in the Post* (Macmillan and The Post Office)
Zilliacus, L.: *From Pillar to Post* (Heinemann)

In addition, various attractive booklets and posters can be
obtained from The Schools Officer, Post Office Headquarters,
St Martins-Le-Grand, London E.C.1.

## PRESENTATION
At the beginning of the assembly set the scene for the series and
the particular programme that day, and introduce the visitor. It
often helps a visitor to get used to the situation to take the spotlight
away from him. The singing of a song is a useful device for this
purpose. The song should have as much relevance as possible to the
theme for the day, in this case, communication. The postman
might even (with a little help from you) point out the connection
between the communication in song that they have all been engaged
in, and his work of conveying written messages.

The postman might like to tell the children about a typical day's
work, mentioning aspects they will be quite familiar with —
collecting and delivering letters — as well as the work that goes on
behind the scenes at the sorting office.

If the guest is a little hesitant about giving a talk, he might prefer
to be interviewed by you or a panel of children from the class
carrying out the study. The children should prepare in advance the
questions they are going to ask. There should also be an opportunity
for children in the audience to ask questions.

Encourage the postman to relate any amusing or unusual
incidents, such as how he deals with fierce dogs, wet days, or heavy
loads at Christmas. These will all help to make valuable points. While
one does not want to overplay the difficulties of any job, it is
important to provide a true picture of what the occupation entails.

## SUPPORT MATERIALS
As well as the books and posters already mentioned, any work the
children have done in their study of the post office could be
exhibited. The classroom pillar box or post office counter (adapted
from the school shop) would provide a suitable background.

Before or after the postman's visit show a film about the work of
the post office. *The Postal Service* and *The Postman* (both Rank
Films) are appropriate, and *Night Mail* (B.I.F.) still carries its years
well.

## DEVELOPMENTS

Classes can make a study of the postman

Send a letter of thanks to the postman, most appropriately, through the mail.

Invite the postman for a return visit to see the development of the children's work.

Small groups can make the following excursions and report back at a later assembly. Be sure to arrange your visit in advance with the appropriate post office officials.

Visit the local sorting office to see what goes on behind the scenes. Ask for a letter handed in at the sorting office to be passed through the system for delivery the next day; visit the post office to see what other work it does (choose a slack time for maximum attention).

Stamp collections can be put on display and a swopping service might be set up.

Set up a temporary post office in the school for the collection and delivery of internal mail for the duration of a project, with one class of children collecting, sorting and delivering letters.

Set up a savings bank at the school. Advice on how to set up such an enterprise can be obtained from the National Savings Movement, Alexandra House, Kingsway, London W.C.2.

Plan lessons on letter writing and envelope addressing.

## THEMES FOR SIMILAR TREATMENT

Policeman, fireman, ambulance driver
Doctor, dentist, nurse
Veterinary surgeon, RSPCA or PDSA official
Baker, butcher, grocer, etc.
Roadsweeper, refuse collector
Farmer, fisherman, forester - if such activities go on in the neighbourhood.
The people within the school: the schoolkeeper, secretary, helpers, cook, cleaners, etc.

A homehelp, matron of an old people's home
A blind person with his guide dog, a disabled person
An elderly person who has lived in the neighbourhood a long time
A welfare officer
A member of a task force team of a housing organisation like Shelter

# IN SEARCH OF A SAINT

Most people, certainly most children, like to have some kind of group identity and something or somebody to symbolise it. Almost all of our church schools have a close link with a particular church. They bear the same dedication and have a celebration day designated to that saint.

A school in the state system might find it interesting to develop an assembly around a saint. You might find that a particular saint can be linked with your school. Celebration of that saint's day every year soon takes its place in the folklore of the school.

## BACKGROUND INFORMATION

I copied down this definition of a saint that I found in an old magazine some years ago.

> **Why were saints, saints?** Because they were cheerful when it was difficult to be cheerful; patient when it was difficult to be patient, because they pushed when they might have wanted to stand still, and kept silent when they might have wanted to be disagreeable.

Cousins, Mary: *Tell Me About The Saints* (Hutchinson)
Brother, Kenneth: *Saints of the Twentieth Century* (Mowbrays)
Windham, Joan: *Here Are your Saints;*
   *Saints by Request;*
   *Saints for all Seasons;*
   *Saints Specially for Boys;*
   *Saints Specially for Girls;*
   *Sixteen Saints for Six O'Clock* (Sheed & Ward)

The stories of saints are sometimes featured in children's papers and church magazines. A church guide often gives information about the saint to whom the church is dedicated.

Where a school has decided to associate itself permanently with a particular saint, research can be engaged in over a number of years to add to the material that can be used during the annual celebration. Thus it was that my own school, Boxgrove, took to itself Saint Blaise, to whom the church in the Sussex village of Boxgrove is dedicated. I wrote briefly about this in *The Book of Festivals* (Mills and Boon) and in the *Church Times*. As a result, I had correspondence that added to our information and, in a number of cases, allowed us to pass back some of our findings to other people doing similar research.

I have used St Blaise as an example in the following sections to give some indication of the kind of material that can be collected, and how it can be used.

## ST BLAISE - BACKGROUND INFORMATION
Blaise, a bishop in Armenia, was martyred in the early part of the fourth century. Before his death he cured a sick child of a serious throat infection and was able to persuade a wolf to release a pig that it had captured. In an effort to get him to renounce God, Blaise was tortured with long woolcombs. Accordingly, he is revered by various groups of people. He became a patron saint of animals and children, but is best known as the patron saint of throat sufferers and woolcombers. He is shown variously with crossed candles at his throat or holding a woolcomb. His special day is February 3.

Dedications at Shanklin, Isle of Wight; St Blazey, Cornwall; Milton, Berkshire; Newton Abbot, Devon; Boxgrove, Sussex. Numerous chapels in cathedrals and churches.

Numerous inns were formerly (and unusually) named after the Bishop, especially in areas associated with the wool trade. There was a very unusual inn in London called Bishop Blaise and the Two Sawyers, which served as a marriage shop 1734–1749. There are inns named after St Blaise still licensed at Andover, Romsey, Exeter and Richmond (Yorkshire). All the landlords wrote back to provide information about their 'dedication'.

There was even a tobacco named Bishop Blaze manufactured by W.D. & H.O. Wills ( and three other firms in the nineteenth century) and distributed particularly in the wool-producing areas of England.

St Blaise has links with European countries; staff and friends visiting Yugoslavia have sent postcards and gathered information.

The Royal National Throat, Nose and Ear Hospital holds an annual ceremony in honour of St Blaise. There are also annual ceremonies in many Catholic churches and schools, e.g. St Blaise Roman Catholic Secondary School, Bradford, and St Blazey School, Par, Cornwall. St Ethelreda's Church, Ely Place, Holborn, London has made available leaflets, medallions and candles of St Blaise.

Libraries in Norwich, Northampton and Bradford sent photostats of newspapers reporting on St Blaise Day parades. Local newspapers in Exeter and Chichester gathered material from readers.

**PRESENTATION**
On or near February 3

A telling of the story of St Blaise

Reading greetings from vicars at the churches of the same dedication. (We hope to have one of them visit us one day.)

A pageant of St Blaise. Details are taken from archive materials. Everyone can take part in the procession

A recital of one of a number of narrative poems about St Blaise, which were written to celebrate the public holiday in the woollen towns in previous centuries

Interludes to tell the story of Jason and the Golden Fleece (he appears in all the eighteenth and nineteenth century parades).

Blessing of throats ceremony by a vicar

A service in church, inform parents beforehand and invite them to attend.

Prayers composed by the children, especially of the type expressing their concern for those suffering from throat complaints.

(Teachers, particularly in their first year, would be grateful for intercedence in this area.) Keep thoughts and prayers for use in future ceremonies.

## SUPPORT MATERIALS
Woolcombs were always a feature of pictures and models of St Blaise, and we were able to borrow a pair from the Castle Museum, York.

Model of St Blaise using wooden armature, chicken wire and papier mâché.

Mosaic picture of St Blaise, using coloured paper pieces torn from magazines.

Communal mural showing the parade; so many figures are required that a general invitation can be made to everyone to add to the scene.

Costumes and props for a play or pageant on the life of the saint.

Make a film of the life of St Blaise for use on some of the celebration occasions.

Series of slides showing St Blaise associations at home and abroad.

Hymns:  *For All the Saints, Who From Their Labours Rest, When The Saints Go Marching In*

Occasionally there may be a hymn written specially for a particular feast day. One of the Blaise churches had such a composition and was pleased to share it with us. It is sung to the tune of 'Southwell'.

> From Scottish Isle*, in bygone days,
> To fair Ragusa town
> The people knew and loved Saint Blaise,
> And held him in renown.

* Pladda, an islet south of Arran. Here, and in Ragusa, Saint Blaise was the Patron Saint.

Our Saint became, so legends say,
The Bishop of Sebaste;
But oft he wished to go away,
To meditate and fast.

While in a mountain cave, he spent
Much time in thought and prayer;
He cured sick beasts, who thither went,
Forgetting every fear.

Saint Blaise was seized, his body scored;
He suffered with each breath:
Courageously he served his Lord,
And died a martyr's death.

O God, we praise Thee for his life;
And pray that Thou wilt send
Such grace, that we, through calm and strife
Keep faithful to the end.

Compose a hymn especially for the occasion and saint, write
new words to fit a well-known tune, or modify a hymn to make
it more appropriate.

## DEVELOPMENTS

Excursions to places associated with the particular saint

Written record of the assembly for the school archives

Writing letters thanking people for their help in supplying
information about the saint

Set up a fund for local or national help

Project by the class or school stimulated by the assembly; for
example, in the case of St Blaise, the story of wool

## THEMES FOR SIMILAR TREATMENT

Other saints:
St David (March 1)
St Patrick (March 17)

St George (April 23)
St Andrew (November 30)
— all opening up the possibilities of national music, poetry, stories, etc.

Saints with particular dedications in the area.

Little-known saints about whom there are interesting stories. St Cadoc is one of my favourites; by his help and that of a mouse, a village was saved from famine.

# TODAY WE ARE GOING TO CELEBRATE GURU NANAK'S BIRTHDAY

Many schools have children from different races, cultures and religions. Their faiths should be respected within an assembly. Themes of common concern to people of all faiths can be explored, and where prayers are used, appropriate ones from the different faiths can be selected and credited. The exploration of different religions can be attempted with children nine years old and up, and older children are surprisingly interested in this field. *World Religions: Aids for Teachers,* published by the Community Relations Commission for the Shap Working Party (10–12 Russell Square, London W.C.1) is an essential directory for anyone attempting such a programme.

Assemblies can also be built around a particular religion when a substantial number of children in the school follow that faith. Such an assembly should go far to increase understanding of, and respect for, other people. If the parents can become involved too, then community relations will also benefit.

There are 80 000 Sikhs in the United Kingdom. There are about 500 in Dundee and 12 000 in Birmingham. Schools in areas with a large Sikh community might like to organise an assembly, festival or celebration on one of the following occasions:
    Baisakhi: held on April 13 or 14, the Sikh New Year
    Guru Nanak's birthday: November 10, birthday of the founder of the Sikh religion
    Guru Gobind Singh: December 24, the Tenth Guru's birthday

## BACKGROUND INFORMATION

The Sikh religion stems from the teachings of Guru Nanak (1469–1539). There were ten gurus in all. A Sikh is one who believes in them and the authority of the Guru Granth Sahib, which is the Holy Book. This book is considered the living embodiment of the gurus and, as such, is reverently treated at all times. It is carried with great ceremony, attended by five sword bearers, and the space around it is whisked clean. After use it is carefully wrapped up and put to bed at night.

The main tenets of the religion are work, worship and charity. The true Sikh practises this triumvirate of ideals in his daily life. All Sikh men take the name Singh as a sign of their common brotherhood. All Sikh women are given the name Koli, which means princess, and they keep this name even after marriage. There are five articles that are sacred to the Sikhs. These are known as the five K's.

## PRESENTATION
The size of the Sikh community within the school will reflect the size of the adult group living in the neighbourhood. Perhaps it would be possible to invite an adult to come and speak about his particular faith for a short time.

The five articles sacred to the Sikh could be shown and spoken about.

> **Kanga** (comb), symbolising cleanliness. Men and boys wear turbans to cover their hair, which is tied in a bun on top of the head.
> **Kesh** (untrimmed hair)
> **Kirpan** (two-edged sword), a symbol of dignity, which will be unsheathed when affairs are past other remedies
> **Kara** (steel bangle), worn by men and women on the right wrist. Symbolises the unity of God and reminds the wearer that he should commit no misdeed with his hand.
> **Kachcha**, short pair of undertrousers

The life story of Guru Nanak could be dramatised.

Another story, the founding of the new order Khalsa, could also be dramatised. In this, the Guru Gobind Singh demanded the head of one of his followers. One man volunteered, and went to the Guru's tent. The sword was heard to fall. With a sword dripping in blood, Guru Gobind Singh came out and demanded the head of another volunteer. Five men in all volunteered and went into the Guru's tent. Then the tent flap was opened and five men came out each bearing a beheaded goat. These five became the first baptised members of the new community (compare Abraham and Isaac).

There are always five warriors with swords unsheathed at the main services at the Sikh temples.

A Sikh wedding could be enacted, with advice from a member of the community.

A Sikh family could be shown going through their daily routine.

A feature of the Sikh assembly could be the sharing of the common meal. Apart from the charitable element, it also breaks down any class or caste attitudes. A small amount of shared food would be most appropriate. The sight and smells of Indian food would engage other senses at the assembly.

There is a considerable amount of background literature. Some of it could be used to make up a temporary resource corner to satisfy some of the curiosity that, one hopes, is aroused after such an assembly, or series of assemblies. These and other publications can be obtained from Luzac & Co. Ltd., 46 Great Russell Street, London, W.C.1.

Cole, W. Owen: *A Sikh Family in Britain* (Religious Education Press)
*Learning for Living,* May, 1973 issue
McLeod, W.H.: *Sikhs of the Punjab* (Graphic Educational Publications)
Parrinder, E.G.: *Sikhism* (in the *Encyclopaedia of World Religions*) (Hamlyn)
Singh, Khushwant; *The Sikhs Today* (Orient Longmans)
Singh, Sihal: *Guru Nanak* (Guru Nanak Foundation)
*Stories from Sikh History* (Hemkunt Press, India - 6 books)
Wylam, Pam: *Guru Nanak* (Childrens' Book Trust, New Delhi)

There are a number of periodicals that are of interest:
*The Sikh Courier; The Sikh Review; The Spokesman Weekly.*

## SUPPORT MATERIALS

Clothes and other articles from the Sikh community
Ornaments and jewellery and pictures of Sikhs

Demonstration of how to tie a turban
Model of the Golden Temple of Amritsar.

Guides: *Hymns at the Conclusion of the Sikh Service; The Sikh Marriage Service*

Records: all available from the Indian Record House, 70 South Road, Southall, Middlesex.
*Guru Nanak Shabads* (ECLP 244)
*Japji and Raheras* (ECLP 2355)
*Asa-di-War* (ECLP 2307 and 2308)
*Sukhmani* (ECLP 2320 and 2321)

Slides: Two sets of slides on Sikh buildings are available from Bury Peerless, 22 Kings Road, Minnis Bay, Birchington, Kent.

Film: *Guru Gobind Singh,* available from India House.

Filmstrips:
*The Sikh Religion,* with taped commentary (Concordia, 117–123 Golden Lane, London, E.C.1)
*The Sikhs* (Educational Productions)
*Sikh Amrit* (Educational Productions)

Tape: *Sikh Service* (in English) try Indian Record House.

## USEFUL ADDRESSES

The Sikh Cultural Society, 88 Mollison Way, Edgware, London HA8 5QW
Sikh Information Centre, 16 Sholebroke Place, Leeds (send a stamped, addressed envelope)
Sikh Missionary Society, 27 Pier Road, Gravesend, Kent
Sikh Temple, Norland Road, Queensdale Road, London W.11.
Sikh Temple, 79 Sinclair Road, London W.14
The International Department of the Christian Education Movement. See p. 114 (For information and copy of Probe No. 14 – *Community Relations*).
The Community Relations Commission, 10-12 Great Russell Street, Russell Square, London W.C.1. (For details of the Shap Working Party and its regular issues of *Aids for World Religions,* including festival dates, etc.)

Yorkshire Committee for Community Relations, Charlton House,
Hamlet Road, Leeds LS10 1EH (especially for booklet
*Religion in the Multifaith School,* edited by W. Owen Cole,
which contains details of Sikh assemblies).

## DEVELOPMENTS

A study of the Sikh community in Britain
A study of the Sikh community in the Punjab
An annual festival
A visit to a Sikh temple

## THEMES FOR SIMILAR TREATMENT

Festivals or assemblies featuring other world religions, Hinduism,
Buddhism, Islam, Judaism, etc (See particularly, *A Book of World
Religions* by E.G. Parrinder, published by Hulton Press.)

# WHAT ABOUT THE OTHER DAYS?

It will be quite evident to everyone reaching this point in the book
that the writer is a firm believer in the need for preparation if the
assembly is to make a substantial impact. It will also be obvious
that since preparation means work, and work means time as well
as inspiration, some types of assembly will not be daily occurrences;
nor should they be. We all know the dangers of too rich a diet.
So what of those other days?

1 You are not the only one who has to, or can, take an assembly.
  Discuss the matter at a staff meeting and arrange a rota. This
  consultation is real participation and also valuable training
  for further responsibility.
2 The BBC broadcasts weekly services for schools. Accompanying
  pamphlets give information on the content, prayers and hymns
  and, often, the introductory music. Suggestions for development
  are also given. Take time to read these notes so that you can
  introduce the service or comment on it after the broadcast.
  Discuss the broadcast with the assembly. Try to explore the
  relevance of the broadcast to the school, local community,
  or a topical news item.
3 Other broadcasts that could be tape-recorded, for use in an
  assembly include: 'Pause for Thought' at 8.45 a.m. on Radio 2,
  or 'Thought for the Day' at 7.45 a.m. on Radio 4. Occasionally
  these talks are brought together by the BBC in modestly-priced
  pamphlets, as, for example, was the 'Pause for Thought' series,
  and 'For Someone Else's Son', which was culled from a series
  on BBC 'Woman's Hour'. Selected items from each week's
  series of 'Woman's Hour' are broadcast on Saturday afternoons
  on Radio 4.
4 If the BBC have repeats, so can you. Keep your assembly notes
  in a drawer, on a shelf, or in a file. Look through them to find
  material appropriate to an assembly that went well on a
  previous occasion.
  You always know when an assembly has been well received.
  If it didn't go well and you feel that the basic material was really

good, try to analyse the weaknesses of the presentation. You might then be able to present the same material in a different, and better, form on another occasion.

If you have the energy and the type of tidy mind needed, you might spend a wet holiday preparing a cross-referenced directory of themes, stories, quotations and anecdotes that could be used to create a variety of assemblies. Has a computer ever been used for this type of instant assembly? What about making a 'Dial an assembly' device, with a series of slots showing hymn references, prayers or readings, and other resources? A diagram and instructions for making a dial are on pages 96–97.

5 What about other heads or teachers in nearby schools? An exchange system of assembly speakers is an idea we can borrow from the world of Sunday schools. At consultative meetings and other more informal gatherings take the names of teachers who would respond to an invitation. You might find yourself repaying the service.

6 Invite vicars, curates, and other churchmen and women to visit the school and join in an assembly. You might want to reserve the invitations for special occasions, such as school anniversaries, harvest festivals, Christmas celebrations, and so on. Discuss the idea with your colleagues. Perhaps some of them will know a clergyman who is particularly skilful at establishing a rapport with young people. Ask clergymen from various faiths and denominations, including the Salvation Army, Church Army, etc. There may be an opportunity to invite a churchman visiting the area to visit the school. When David Shepherd, Bishop of Woolwich was on a visit to Abbey Wood, he enjoyed visiting our school and speaking during the assembly. When our school had a festival on Scandinavia, the pastor from the Norwegian Church in Rotherhithe accepted an invitation to speak to us. Details of the numbers and age range of the children, and usual forms of assembly should be given to the speaker in advance. Perhaps you can tactfully suggest the theme currently being explored at the school. You might indicate ways in which the children could participate, listing hymns and songs they know, or dances or a playlet that they might prepare. Also discuss any other aids available, such as records, projectors and so on. Telephone or write to your guest just a few days before the assembly to ensure that the engagement has not been overlooked, and to confirm the time and provide clear travelling directions.

Visitors usually welcome coffee or other refreshment with the staff. If the assembly has been successful, return visits by the guest will appeal to the children. 'How long shall I speak for? asked one vicar. 'Oh, about ten minutes', I suggested. 'Ten minutes, then', he said. And he kept his promise. He'll be back. If a visit to a church or outside hall is made, permission should be obtained from parents. Why not invite them to come along too?

7　Ask the children to prepare an assembly. Some of the older pupils at secondary level could certainly manage this task quite easily on their own. It is not an impossible assignment for ten- and eleven-year-olds, but they would probably appreciate having help and advice always at hand.

Children's ideas are valuable too. The section of 'Hands' in the ILEA Agreed Syllabus *Learning for Life* has proved useful to teachers because of the range of ideas it discusses. Yet in ten minutes of discussion with a fourth year group the following ideas emerged: kind hands, healing hands, caressing hands, aggressive hands, fighting hands, grasping hands, begging hands, leprous hands, injured hands, worn hands, pointing hands, appealing hands, waving hands, helping hands, praying hands, blessing hands, skilful hands, lifting hands, rescuing hands, coloured hands, joined hands, talking hands, no hands, stopping hands.

In fact, the suggestions started off a whole series of assemblies and an interesting series of pen and ink sketches inspired by Durer's *Praying Hands.*

8　Look at Resources Directory for a list of assembly anthologies. Examine these off-the-peg collections to see if they fit you and your style. With just a small alteration or two, some may be just right for you to use.

9　This anecdote was one I saved for just the sort of situation where the head suddenly says, 'Something has come up, I can't take assembly. Just you carry on.'

In a particular abbey it was the custom for each of the monks in turn to make an address. These talks were interesting and varied, individual and sincere. Brother Paul was not looking forward to his turn (few really do) and tried all kinds of ploys to avoid the fateful evening — feigning a sore throat, extra work in the kitchen. Finally, the brethren's patience was exhausted.

He stood up. They waited.

'Do you know what I am going to say?' he asked.
'No', they chorused.
'Neither do I,' stammered Paul and sat down.
On the next evening they all insisted that Paul should speak again.
Reluctantly he got to his feet.
'Do you know what I am going to say tonight?' he queried.
Not to be caught out, they all answered 'Yes'
'Then there's no need for me to say it,' said Paul quickly and sat
down on his bench.
On the third night the monks agreed on their strategy, and they
insisted on Paul getting to his feet after the evening meal.
'Brothers, do you know what I am going to say?' he asked yet
again.
'Yes,' said the brothers on the east side of the refectory.
'No,' said the brothers who sat on the west side of the refectory.
'In that case, will those who know, tell those who don't, and that
will save me having to do it,' smiled Paul.
The brothers admitted that they had been bested . . . and then
thought about Paul's words carefully.

10  Make a joyful noise unto the Lord. Gather the community
     together and just sing. The repertoire available to us today is
     wide. You need do no more than give a word of two of
     introduction before each song. A great feeling of happiness
     can spring from this kind of gathering. It's a good way to
     start off the day. One friend of mine always wishes his
     children a happy day at the end of assembly. For them
     the assembly is an important start to the day's activities.

11  Order a film, filmstrip, slide set or audio-visual aid programme
     from one of the organisations listed on pages 113—115. Preview
     the material before the assembly. At the assembly introduce
     it and comment on it afterwards. Some publicity at a previous
     assembly and on a notice-board will help to ensure an
     interested, rather than merely an attending, audience.

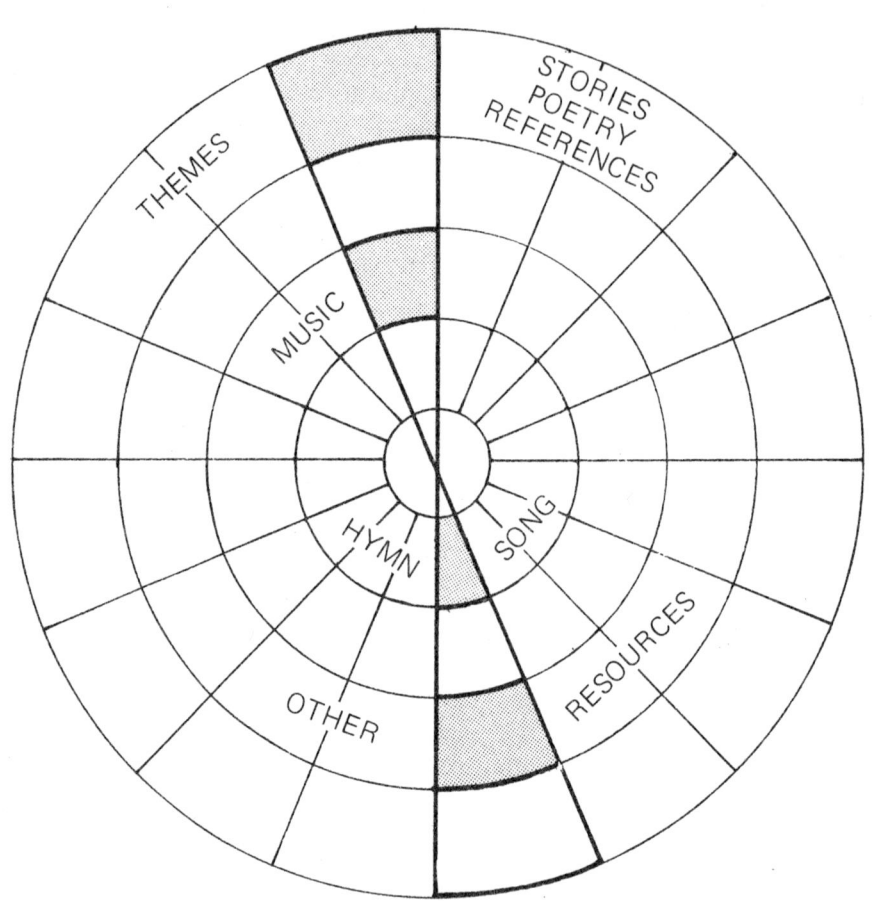

*Dial an assembly*

Prepare *two* card discs 10 cm in radius. Draw concentric rings
on each side of the discs 7,5,3 and 1 cm in radius. Now draw two
diameters set 22.5° apart. Shade alternate sections as in the diagram
and cut these out of both discs.

Because an angle of 22.5° has been chosen, sixteen sectors are possible, but since the gaps will coincide in one position, fifteen areas will be used. By reversing the two discs, which should now be fixed with a paper fastener, thirty assemblies can be programmed on the discs. I have suggested the headings to go alongside the spaces.

Start with the gaps in each disc in line. Move the top disc clockwise until it just closes the gap. Now fill in the details in all four boxes for the assembly you are recording. Draw around the shapes in each case so that the next alignment is easy to achieve. When you have recorded fifteen regular favourite assemblies, reverse the dial and begin another series.

# ASSEMBLY LINES

Over a number of years I have collected ideas for assemblies.
In a way it is rather like beachcombing. But stones, even precious
and semi-precious stones, need shaping, polishing and setting before
they can be seen in all their beauty and varied form.

So do come beachcombing and see if you can find anything you can use.
I have frequently used the association idea. Perhaps you can take some
of the ideas further, and in a different direction. I hope that the plan of
noting down a single and simple idea will appeal to you.

1 A rainy day    Songs about rain – protection from the rain
   (houses, raincoats, wellington boots, umbrellas), clouds (and
   silver linings), measuring rain, places that have too much rain,
   places that do not have enough, the rain cycle, our need for
   water, plants' need for water, Noah and the flood, St Swithin
   and Winchester.
2 Symbols in Compton Church, near Guildford

| | |
|---|---|
| Union and conflict | Stability and change |
| Day and night | Ebb and flow |
| Growth and decay | Life and death |
| Good and evil | Labour and rest |
| Joy and sorrow | Spirit and flesh |
| Real and ideal | Freedom and limits |

These contrasting concepts could form the basis for a term
of assemblies. Introduce each polarisation on Monday morning
and during the week invite some work and discussion.
3 What do you think are the most important things in life?
   Invite as many people as possible to respond to this question –
   the pupils, staff (teaching and non-teaching), parents, managers,
   or governors. Where there may be some reticence, suggest that
   this is done on a question-and-answer basis. Each person can suggest
   music or readings, or show something that comes within the definition
   of the title of the series.

4 Faith, hope and charity (I Corinthians 13: 13) A trio of
assemblies, each one with illustrations. During the darkest days
of the Second World War three old Gladiator aircraft defended
the island of Malta; they were known as Faith, Hope and Charity.
(Anagram: the true meaning of Christianity − it's in charity)
5 The Lord's Prayer taken line by line, at intervals of time.
Sing the Caribbean version of the prayer.
6 The ten commandments one by one, week by week.
7 The human body − various limbs and organs will provide subject
matter for an assembly:
feet, hands, brain, stomach, bones (backbone, wishbone, funnybone,
jawbone − providing some lighthearted treatment). The five senses
can also be taken one by one, with attention given to the absence
or the losing of these − blindness, deafness, etc. Follow-up work
can be done on the work of Dogs for the Blind Association, Royal
National Institute for the Blind, Louis Braille, etc.
Other problems associated with the body − accidents, diseases,
operations, hospitals, nurses, doctors, scientists, charities, safety
rules, fire risks.
8 The family − marriage, birth, growing up, leaving home, old age;
home, sharing, difficulties, relations, neighbours, friends. Private
and government organisations for assisting us when we are in need.
Local branches can be contacted to provide assistance.
9 A series of books can provide the starting point for assembly
themes and background information for the development of a
topic, for example, the *New Citizen* series by Wayland Publishers
Ltd. Titles include: *In Trouble with the Law, Down and Out,
Going into Hospital, Car Smash.* Dramatisation of these themes would be
suitable.
Another useful series is *Changing Scene* from Burke Press.
Titles include: *The By-Pass, The Tower Block, The New Town,
The Branch Line.* Children in urban areas will be aware of many
of the situations described in these books. With assistance from
newspapers, they can show how relevant these issues are locally.
10 The problem of loneliness − contrast with solitude; the plight
of the old, the sick, the abandoned, the stranger, the member
of a minority group. A series of case studies could be created,
with an invitation to provide solutions or at least some
amelioration of the problem. Taken near Christmas or other
occasion for celebration makes such problems more poignant.
11 Uniforms − people who serve us, collection of hats, badges,
and other insignia that help to identify and describe various

occupations and services. An opportunity for groups of children to study the work of one or more of these services and present their report to others.

12 Who cares? A look at the local, national and international scene to find examples of people, organisations, or governments who care about someone else or some situation. Local and national newspapers will provide data for this topic.

13 Judge for yourself — various situations, grievances, arguments can be aired. There is a need to present evidence from both sides, and then leave it to everyone to make up his own mind.

14 People who turned back, changed their mind, reformed, e.g. Dick Whittington, St Paul.

15 Things that are small — unconsidered trifles, simple things small cogs in a large machine, a place for the humble worker — 'If your're a roadsweeper, make sure you are a good one.' The place of a team player; it is interesting to demonstrate how one twig can be broken easily, but how when one puts ten together, it is almost impossible to break the bundle.

A Chinese poem from 2500 BC:

> When the sun rises I go to work.
> When the sun goes down I take my rest.
> I dig the well from which I drink
> I farm the soil that yields my food.
> I share creation. Kings can do no more.

16 Things that are large — great·nations, giants — and those who conquer them — David and Goliath, George and the Dragon, etc.; armies, powerful rulers, champions.

17 What day is it today? Calendars, newspapers, almanacs and diaries will provide references to various anniversaries. Often organisations issue literature concerning a particular day. Some advance work needs to be done if the maximum is to be gained from it. Note local anniversaries and school occasions — someone's birthday perhaps. The first day of term, the last day of term, the last day of the school year, looking forward and backwards.

18 The enemies within — hate, greed, cruelty, jealousy, envy. Illustrate with a story, e.g., greed:

Four beggars lived together in a dark hovel. Each day they went out hoping to beg enough offerings from passers-by to keep themselves fed. One day one was able to obtain some meat, another, some spices, the third, some potatoes and the fourth, some other vegetables. On their return they agreed to make a stew. In their dwelling that evening they set a pot on the fire and filled it with water. Each pretended to put in the contents from his own bowl and gave the mixture a stir. They then sat down to wait. When the cooking time was up, each man ladled some stew into his bowl. They all began to eat and then spat out the water – hot water – for that was all that each had given and all that he had received. They had all been greedy, thinking that they would have a share of the others' food and then sneak off to cook and eat their own. They agreed to start the cooking again, with better results this time.

19 Gold – the greed for gold, gold prospectors, hallmarking, the story of King Midas, gold a gift for Jesus.

20 The Creation – Biblical version, compare it with legends and stories from other cultures. Opportunities for drama, art work.

21 The natural world – the seasons, the beauty of the world, 'Have nothing about you that you do not know to be useful or believe to be beautiful.' (William Morris)
'If you have two loaves, sell one and buy a lily,' (Chinese proverb). The trees and other plants, birds and other animals, animals and plants in school or brought in temporarily from home.
Beautiful days are plentiful – each one can be the subject for an assembly, the shape of leaves, the polish on a stone, the beauty of a feather.

22 Disasters – earthquakes, volcanoes, floods, plagues, famines, droughts, war, civil war. No shortage of examples, sadly, every newspaper and TV news bulletin will provide substance. We need to try to present the facts and, in the case of natural disasters, see if there is anything we can do about them.

23 Remarkable people of today – newspapers, etc., will feature these people, and recent history will provide examples, e.g. wartime pilot Group Captain Cheshire, who founded the Cheshire Homes for the Incurable.

24 Wheels – a thematic approach to provide a sequence of assemblies, transport, journeys, exploration, the spare wheel of a motor car, the Inner Wheel organisation, the story of St Catherine.

25 Those who were first – the pioneers, to sail around the world, go into space, reach the top of Mount Everest, print a book.

26 Crossings – across the Atlantic, across the Equator, across the

English Channel, across the Red Sea, across the road; bridges between groups of people, the *Bridge of San Luis Rey* (by Thornton Wilder). This makes a good topic for class study with examples used for the assembly.

27  The Pilgrim's Progress; refer to John Bunyan, of course, but also *Every Child's Pilgrim's Progress* by Derek McCulloch (Epworth Press) and the relevant section of *Thieves and Angels* by David Holbrook (Cambridge University Press). BBC record *Pilgrim's Progress*, RESRI.
Interesting variation to provide a progress for a modern pilgrim, written and dramatised. Art work and puppetry could feature as well as story telling and dramatic interpretations. A frieze that is built up week by week as the story unfolds would provide the serial appeal. Used in strip cartoon form it would provide opportunity for written work.

28  What's the evidence? The walls of Jericho, the crossing of the Red Sea, the miracle, the Dead Sea Scrolls, who moved the stone? Such situations can be handled in true detective story fashion, with the story being brought forward. See *The Witnesses*, by David Kossoff (Collins) for the use that could be made of this technique. Once again allow the listeners to decide.

29  Rescue — the work of the Royal National Lifeboat Institution, the coastguard, the lighthouse keepers, air-sea rescue, mountain rescue, cave rescue, mining rescue, flood rescue, undersea rescue. The national mass media describe stirring deeds frequently and many of the children will be familiar with at least some of the detail.
Local events will have an impact too, rescue from fires, cats from trees, people in road accidents. This could be tied in with a school project or emphasis on safety. In the primary school it could be linked with a visit by a police road safety team, or a borough exhibition on safety in the home. Again there is a link with hospitals, doctors, nurses, medicine, St John's Ambulance Brigade, etc.

30  The protection of children, children in care, the work of the National Society for the Prevention of Cruelty to children, save the Children Fund, Dr Barnardo's Homes. Links with stories about children from the Bible, Samuel, David, Jesus, Jairus' daughter. A story is told of a new cleaner at Dr Barnardo's old headquarters in Stepney. The founder's study had been kept in its original state and a wax effigy had been placed at the desk. When the cleaner reported to the supervisor, she said she had

swept and dusted, but would have to return to the study later. When she had gone then, it had been occupied. As she told the supervisor, 'The Master is still working'.

31 Protection – tied in with the last two items in many ways – parents, guardians, the law, the police, the army, homes, clothes, rainwear, tools, safety checks, insurance policies, store cupboards.

32 Harvest – how others live, how others die, the farmer, the food chain, natural foods, food from the hedgerow, food from the sea, processing food, cleanliness of food, school dinners, the work of Oxfam.
Between 'harvest' and 'starve' there is only an 'h' – help? heaven? happiness? hunger?
Anybody can be generous in a good fruit year.
Be sure as you've got an orchard, somebody will give you apples.
Gandhi said, 'There are so many hungry people that God cannot appear to them except in the form of bread.'
If you have two loaves sell one and buy a lily (Chinese proverb).
It is interesting to see how items such as this can be used in a number of contexts.

33 Yours sincerely (*sans cere* – without a crack – used to guarantee pottery) – yours faithfully, your obedient servant, yours truly.

34 Power – strength, water power, electrical power, coal, oil, spiritual strength, concerted strength.

35 Sharing – gifts, goodwill, resources, stories, the light from a candle, neighbours, friends.
'I shall pass through the world but once. Any good things therefore that I can do, any kindness I can show my fellow creature, let me do it now. Let me not defer nor neglect it, for I shall not pass this way again'. (Quaker prayer)
Thermotacles, when selling a farm asked the crier to proclaim that among its commodities it had a good neighbour (Plutarch, AD 120).

36 Caring – for the young, the old, each other, animals, for people of a different colour, race, creed, for our enemies. I was angry about not having any shoes, until I met a man without his feet. (Chinese saying). A friend is someone who knows you and still likes you. The children will provide other revealing definitions of friendship.

37 Conservation – preservation, protection, pollution, progress, resources, needs, responsibility, societies and agencies – United Nations, science for peaceful uses.

38 Science – machines, light, sound, chemistry, electricity, power

manufactured, power controlled. Many scientific principles can be simply demonstrated by children to develop this theme, with examples of the way in which particular scientific discoveries and developments have benefited mankind. One or more groups of children could develop this study and provide material for many assemblies (see the series of booklets *Science 5/13* – Macdonald Educational). The other side of the coin can be explored with older children, i.e., the nuclear bomb, nerve gases, weapons of war, scientific devices designed not to save life but to destroy it.

39 People who served mankind – Elizabeth Fry, Florence Nightingale, etc. With older children it is interesting to explore the lives of those who fall within this category, but who may have had a debit side to reveal, e.g. Alfred Nobel.

40 Music – composers, perhaps of the music being used in assembly. Provide details of the lives and illustrate with music.

41 Other countries – information, maps, posters, national costume, examples from their industry, crafts, art, etc., music, folk tales, heroes, beliefs. With international travel as common as it is today, it is possible for a national of almost any foreign country to be in the British Isles. Try universities, polytechnics, travel agents, etc.

42 Temptation – choosing right from wrong, dares, 'chicken', counselling.

43 Holidays – by the sea, in the country, abroad, at home, for the old, for the convalescent, the need for a change. Opportunity for displays; accounts from children about to go on holiday.

44 Stories from the Bible – Jonah, Gideon, Samson, Joshua, David, Ruth, Abraham and Isaac, Cain and Abel.

45 In search of a king – Arthur, Edward the Confessor, Bonnie Prince Charlie; these and many others could prove to be interesting researches and a chance to discover something of the character of the man. The story of Jesus would come within this category and could be timed to run before Christmas, when one is frequently wanting a different approach.

46 The Sun – sun worshippers, life-giving force, plant growth, rain cycle, life cycle, the seasons, day and night, hot countries, deserts, greenhouses, harnessing the power of the sun, converting power.

47 The disciples – how they were chosen, what they did, how they were tested, and how they stood up to difficulties. Character is not made in a crisis – it is revealed.

48 Assembly alphabet – a story a week from the Bible: Adam,

Bartimaeus, Christ, David, Esau. . . .

49 And Jesus said. . . . Use statements from the New Testament and discuss their relevance today, after finding out why, when and how Jesus came to say what he did.

50 A film for assembly — prepare and follow up each showing to obtain the maximum value, e.g., *Two Men and a Wardrobe* (Polanski Films), *Time out of War* (Rank Films).

51 Mountains and the stories behind them — Everest, Vesuvius, Mt Sinai.

52 The sea — fishermen, sailors, adventurers, danger at sea, hardship at sea, famous ships, famous voyages, famous sailors, the harvest of the sea, sea songs, shanties, poems; the work of the harbour pilots; link with a school journey to the sea.

53 This is where I live — results of a study of the environment. Compare the life style of someone in the school with that of a pen-pal from abroad, or compare someone with a relation abroad. Slides, music, film, visitors can be brought in to make this a vivid description. Original writing, tape-recordings, pictures can all be brought into this approach.

54 Enquiry into an injustice — a local case can be used or some international theme, the plight of the gypsies, the closing of a road, the felling of some trees, the eviction of a tenant, the closing of a factory with resultant unemployment, the punishment of a protestor...any of these cases can be handled as a court of enquiry with various people providing evidence. It might even be possible to bring in someone actually involved in the 'case', to put a point of view.

55 Road signs — use as symbols, slow, danger ahead, no overtaking, road narrows, no right turn, etc.

56 TV advertisements — promises, promises; whiter than white, newspaper and billboard hoardings. Put up a series of claims that seem to contradict one another.

57 Protest — see 'Whistleblower' series in the *Observer*, dumping of chemicals, canals going into disrepair, badger-baiting. Other topical issues can be given an airing, e.g., blood sports could take the form of a debate.

58 The plague village of Eyam — see *At the time of the Plague and the Fire*, Geoffrey Middleton (Longman).

59 Interesting people from the Bible, e.g. Zaccheus (see *Learning for Living*, March, 1972, published by S.C.M. Press, for article on children's understanding of the Zaccheus story). Also Simon, Peter, Judas, Barabbas, etc.

60 Great friendships — Ruth and Naomi, David and Jonathan.

61 Things that make me angry — the money changers in the temple made Jesus very angry. Invite people to discuss issues that upset them and what they can do about it.

62 The story of a local charity, e.g., a hospital where a particular service is carried out, or where on a particular day of the year some special provision is made for the poor. (An interesting link can be made with the Maundy Thursday service.)

63 The story of the months, e.g., Janus, the Roman God with two faces who looks back on the old year and forward to the new.

64 The story of the days of the week.

65 People from stories — most people have their favourites, e.g., Abel Magwitch and Ebenezer Scrooge from Dickens (see BBC record *Characters from Dickens,* RESR 16).

66 Miracle and mummers' plays — drama groups in the school might take and study these and present one or more at appropriate seasons.

67 Colours — the association of colour, red for danger, white for purity, etc.

68 Me
    When I was young, I tried to reform the world.
    When I grew older, I tried to reform my country.
    When I grew older still, I tried to reform my town.
    When I grew yet older, I tried to reform my friends.
    Now as I near the end of my life, I am trying to reform myself.

    Just be yourself — and you will be someone.
    When you point a finger at someone, there are three fingers pointing back at you.
    If you were on trial for being a Christian, would you be found guilty?
    The real enemy is within oneself.

69 What does your dad do? People in the community can be invited to talk about their work and the contribution they make to society.

70 Our school — go back in the school archives and log books to see what incidents have affected the school. Old pupils or former members of staff might be available to come to the assembly.

# Part 3

# INTRODUCTION

The subjects of religious education, moral education and assemblies have been matters of increasing interest in recent years. As a direct result of this, the available resources have increased accordingly, and within this section of the book I have attempted to put them into some kind of order so that when aid is required in a particular area, the reader can quickly find help.

Frequently, book and other exhibitions adopt a special theme, and the subject of interest to us takes its turn with others. If it has not been used recently at your regional gathering, why not suggest it to the organisers? If there is an active teachers' centre in your neighbourhood, why not set up an exhibition of Assembly Resources or have an Assembly Workshop, at which a display of materials and suitable support aids could be a feature?

A number of resource centres have been set up in various parts of the country, some financed by the LEA's and others by Church Education Departments, e.g. Gloucester Diocese Resource Centre; St. Mary's Centre, Reading; Homerton College, Cambridge; the National Catechetical Centre, 15 Denbigh Road, London, W.11.; R.E. and In-Service Training and Resource Centre, West London Institute of Higher Education, Borough Road, Isleworth; West Hill College R.E. Resources and In-Service Training Centre, Alana Geale House, Kingswood Close, Westhill College, Selly Oak, Birmingham. The National Society have two centres; one at The College, Lord Mayor's Walk, York, and the other at 23 Kensington Square, London W8. The Westminster R.E. Centre (Roman Catholic) is also at this address. In all cases it is better to make an appointment with the Director of the Centre concerned.

The Christian Education Movement, 2 Chester House, Pages Lane, London N.10, have an extensive range of publications and other resources which would be particularly valuable to primary and middle school teachers, and headteachers preparing assemblies. There is a Primary Adviser on the staff at C.E.M. Issue No 7 of their Primary School Scheme deals with school assemblies; No 8 offers helpful advice on traditional stories and story telling.

# 1 INFORMATION AND AIDS

## BOOKS AND PUBLICATIONS ABOUT ASSEMBLIES IN SCHOOLS

These are useful to read in connection with planning and philosophy of assemblies.

*Assemblies in Schools* (I.L.E.A.)

Baynes, K. and K.: *Worship* (Lund Humphries)

Brophy, B.: *Religious Education in State Schools* (Fabian Tract 374)

Bruce, V. and Tooke, J.: *Lord of the Dance* (Pergamon)

Copley, T & G.: *First School R.E.* (S.C.M.)

Cox, E.: *Changing Aims in Religious Education* (Routledge and Kegan Paul)

Dean, Joan: *Religious Education for Children* (Ward Lock Educational)

Fourth, R.: *The Durham Report (Religion and Moral Education in County Schools)* (S.P.C.K.)

Goldman, R.: *Religious Thinking from Childhood to Adolescence* (Routledge and Kegan Paul)

Hood, G.: *Festivals* (Religious Education Press)

Hull, J.: *Worship and the Curriculum* (Journal of Curriculum Studies, Vol. I No. 3; November, 1969)

Jasper, Tony: *Sounds Seventies* (Galliard)

Jones, A. and Bottrey, J.: *Children and Stories* (Blackwell)

Jones, C.E.M.: *Worship in the Secondary School* (Pergamon)

Jones, C.M.: *School Worship* (University of Leeds, Paper no. 3)

Kent, Sister Mary Corita, Cox, Harvey and Eisenstein, S.E.: *Play, Pray Book* (Pilgrim Press, Philadelphia)

Konstant, D.: *Syllabus for R.I. for Catholic Primary and Secondary Schools* (Darton, Longman and Todd)

Madge, V.: *Children in Search of Meaning* (S.C.M.)

Tooke, J.: *Religious Studies* (Blond Educational)

Walton, R.C.: *A Source Book of the Bible for Teachers* (SCM)

Waters, D.: *Book of Festivals; A Book of Celebrations* (Mills and Boon)

Wilkes, Keith: *Worship in Assembly* (Learning for Living, November, 1970)
*Prospects and Problems for R.E.* (Department of Education and Science, HMSO)

A useful film, *Of Primary Concern,* can be hired from the National Society for Religious Education, 69 Great Peter Street, London S.W.1.

## BOOKS ABOUT DRAMA AND MOVEMENT WORK

Addison, R.: *Children Make Music* (Holmes-McDougall)
Adland, D.E.: *The Group Approach To Drama* (4 Vols)(Longman)
Barnfield, Gabriel: *Creative Drama in Schools* (Macmillan Ed.)
Billing, R.N.P. and Clegg, J.D.: *Teaching Drama* (U.L.P.)
Caldwell, H.: *The Play Way* (Heinemann)
City of Birmingham Education Committee: *Living Together* (City of Birmingham)
Gray, V. and Percival, R.: *Music, Movement and Mime* (O.U.P.)
Hodgson, J. and Richards, E.: *Living Expression* (Ginn)
Love, M.: *Let's Dramatise* (Chester House)
Martin, William and Vallins, Gordon.: *Exploration Drama* (4 Vols) (Evans)
Massialas, B.G. and Zenn, J.: *Creative Encounters in the Classroom* (J. Wiley and Sons)
Russell, Joan: *Creative Dance in the Primary School* (Macdonald and Evans)
Silks, G. and Dunnington, H.: *Children's Theatre and Creative Dramatics* (Harper and Row)
Slade, P.: *An Introduction to Child Drama; Child Drama* (U.L.P.)
Slater, W.: *Teaching Modern Educational Dance* (Macdonald and Evans)
Tillman, J.: *Exploring Sound* (Galliard)
Tooke, J.D. and Bruce, V.: *Lord of the Dance* (Pergamon)
*Drama in Education,* Vol 1—No 3 *English in Education* (Bodley Head)

## MAGAZINES, JOURNALS AND OCCASIONAL PAPERS
These contain articles about assemblies; reviews of books and other aids, ideas on experimental worship, etc.

*Today* monthly magazine; Circulation Manager, Church House, Dean's Yard, London SW1P 3NZ

*British Journal of Religious Education* (C.E.M.)

*Spectrum* a magazine for Christians in education; 47 Marylebone Lane, London W.1.

*Probe* three times a year; specialised theme chosen for each issue (C.E.M.)

*AVA Magazine* for religious education topics; contains articles reviews, details of equipment, etc.; 2 Eaton Gate, London S.W.1

*AERA Bulletin* World Education Fellowship; Highcroft House, Crown Lane, Sutton Coldfield, Warwickshire.

*Journal of Moral Education* biannual; Pemberton Publishing Co.

*Lumen Vitae* quarterly; magazine for Roman Catholic teachers

*Christian Drama* Religious Drama Society of Great Britain, George Bell House, Bishops Hall, Ayres Street, Southwark, London S.E.1

*Shap News* world religions; Department of Religious Studies, Borough Road College, Isleworth, Middlesex

*The New Era* Yew Tree Cottage, Five Ashes, Mayfield, Sussex

*Sack Magazine* Community Service Volunteers, 237 Pentonville Road, London N1 9NJ or 27 Queen Street, Edinburgh 2.

*Buzz Magazine* 86 Burlington Road, New Malden, Surrey

*The New Sower* Mayhew-McCrimmon, Gt. Wakering, Essex

## BOOKS RELATING TO AUDIO-VISUAL AIDS

The use of audio-visual aids is so much part of the learning situations in classrooms today it is surprising that we don't make greater use of them in the assembly hall. Sometimes we may be unaware of the potential of a piece of hardware, or the availability of the appropriate software, while in other cases we may be completely unfamiliar with a particular machine.

Here is a short list of publications that should inform and stimulate. While some books deal with the whole range of hardware, others - as will be seen from their particular titles - concentrate on a particular machine or aspect of audio-visual education.

Atkinson, N.: *Modern Teaching Aids* (Applied Science Publishers)

Beal, J.D.: *How to make Films at School* (Focal Press)

Beaumont-Craggs, R.: *Slide Tape and Dual Projection* (Focal Press)

Beeby, A.E.: *Sound Effects on Tape* (Print and Press Ltd.)

Coppen, Helen: *Aids to Teaching and Learning* (Pergamon); Wall Sheets (NCVAE)

Hilliard, R.L.: *Radio Broadcasting* (Focal Press)

Jones, J.G.: *Teaching with Tape* (Focal Press)
Kingdon, J.M.: *A Classified Guide to Sources of Educational Film Material* (NCVAE)
Lloyd, J.: *The All-In-One Tape Recorder Book* (Focal Press)
Powell, L.S.: *Guide to the Overhead Projector; Guide to the Use of Visual Aids* (BACIE)
Romiszowski, A.J.: *Selection and Use of Instructional Media* (Kogan Page)
Weston, J.: *The Tape Recorder in the Classroom* (NCVAE)
Wright, A.: *Producing Slides and Filmstrips* (Kodak)

While the effect of the use of a sound or visual effect in assembly can be striking and memorable, mistakes are easily made and the atmosphere ruined. Machines and the use of aids should be carefully prepared in advance for the best results.

## MAGAZINES AND JOURNALS RELATING TO AUDIO-VISUAL AIDS

*Visual Education* monthly magazine; National Committee for Visual Aids in Education (NCVAE). The Year Book, issued in July, is particularly helpful with its lists of materials sources, reading matter, etc.
*AVA Magazine* 2 Eaton Gate, London S.W.1
*Audio Visual* (Maclaren)
*Look and Listen* monthly (Hansom Books)
*Records and Recording* monthly (Hansom Books)
*Sight and Sound* quarterly (British Film Institute)
*Tape Teacher* (3M United Kingdom, 3M house, Wigmore Street, London W1A 1ET)

The annual exhibition, InterNavex, held in recent years in July at Olympia is a splendid showcase for all the latest developments in this field.

## MAILING LISTS

Where it is envisaged that regular use will be made of films and other audio visual aids, it is a good idea to be put on the various mailing lists issued by the various organisations, so that catalogues and other announcements are received regularly.

Association of Teachers of R.E. in Scottish Schools, I Lammermuir Place, Kirkcaldy.

Association for Religious Education, 8 Ninfield Road, Acocks Green, Birmingham.

Association of Christian Teachers, 47 Marylebone Lane, London W.1

Baptist Missionary Society, 93 Gloucester Place, London W.1

Bible Lands Society, The Old Kiln, Hazelmere, High Wycombe, Buckinghamshire

Bible Reading Fellowship, 2 Elizabeth Street, London S.W.1

BBC TV Enterprises, 85-129 Oundle Road, Peterborough, Northants

British and Foreign Bible Society, 146 Queen Victoria Street, London E.C.4

British Council of Churches, 10 Eaton Gate, London S.W.1

British Film Institute, 8 Dean Street, London W.1

British Transport Films, Melbury Terrace, London N.W.1

Camera Talks, 31 North Road, London W.1

Carwal Audio-Visual Aids, P.O. Box 55, Wallington, Surrey

Catholic Institute for International Relations, Ed. Dept., 1 Cambridge Terrace, London N.W.1

Central Film Library, Bromyard Avenue, London, W.3

Christian Aid, 240-250 Ferndale Road, Brixton, London S.W.9

Christian Education Movement, 2 Chester House, Muswell Hill, London N.10

Church Army, CSC House, North Circular Road, London N.W.10

Church Missionary Society, 157 Waterloo Road, London S.E.1

Common Ground (Longmans) ESA, Pinnacles, Harlow, Essex

Concord Film Council, Nacton, Ipswich, Suffolk

Concordia Films, 117-123 Golden Lane, London E.C.1

Congregational Council for World Mission, 11 Carteret Street, London S.W.1

Council for Education in World Citizenship, 93 Albert Embankment, London S.E.1

Educational Productions, Bradford Road, East Ardsley, Wakefield, Yorkshire

Fact and Faith Films, 37 Coton Road, Nuneaton, Warwicks.

Gateway Educational Media, St. Lawrence House, 29/31 Broad Street, Bristol

Guild Sound and Vision, Woodston House, 85-129 Oundle Road, Peterborough, Northants

Hulton Educational Publications Ltd., Raans Road, Amersham, Bucks

Methodist Division of Education and Youth, 2 Chester House, Pages Lane, Muswell Lane, Muswell Hill, London N.10

Methodist, Church Overseas Division, 25 Marylebone Road, London N.W.1

National Audio-Visual Aids Centre, 254-6 Belsize Road, London N.W.6

National Catechetical Centre, 13-15 Denbigh Road, Notting Hill Gate, London W.11
National Christian Education Council, Robert Denholm House, Nutfield, near Redhill, Surrey
Notting Hill Ecumenical Centre, 35 Jermyn Street, London S.W.1
Pictorial Charts Education Trust, 27 Kirchen Road, London W.13
Presbyterian Bookshop, Teaching Aids Dept., Fisherwick Place, Belfast
Rank Film Library, P.O. Box 70, Great West Road, Brentford, Middlesex
Religious Films Ltd., Foundation House, Walton Road, Watford
Scottish Council for Educational Technology, 16-17 Woodside Terrace, Glasgow G3
Scripture Union, 5 Wigmore Street, London, W.1
Society for Promoting Christian Knowledge, Holy Trinity Church, Marylebone Road, London N.W.1
United Society for Christian Literature, Luke House, Farnham Road, Guildford, Surrey
United Society for the Propagation of the Gospel, 15 Tufton Street, London S.W.1
World Congress of Faiths, 23 Norfolk Square, London W.2


## USEFUL ORGANISATIONS

A number of organisations concerned with relief, charity, housing aid etc., have education and information departments which disseminate various kinds of aids that will be useful when work associated with their purpose is being carried out in class, and which would form the basis for assemblies.

British Humanist Association, 13 Prince of Wales Terrace, London W.8
British Red Cross Society, 9 Grosvenor Crescent, London S.W.1
Catholic Institute for International Relations, 1 Cambridge Terrace, London N.W.1
Christian Aid, 2 Sloane Gardens, London W.1
Community Relations Commission, 15 Bedford Street, London W.C.2
Council for Education in World Citizenship, 93 Albert Embankment, London S.E.1
Dr. Barnardo's Homes, Tanners Lane, Barkingside, Essex
Help The Aged, 8 Denman Street, London S.W.1
The National Secular Society, 698 Holloway Road, London N.19
Oxfam, 274 Banbury Road, Oxford

Pestalozzi Children's Village Trust, 81 High Street, Battle, Sussex
Salvation Army, 101 Queen Victoria Street, London E.C.4
Save The Children Fund, 157 Clapham Road, London S.W.9
UNICEF, 46 Osnaburgh Street, London N.W.1
Voluntary Committee on Overseas Aid and Development, Parnell
    House, Wilton Road, London S.W.1
War on Want, 467 Caledonian Road, London N.7

Details of the VENISS Scheme can be obtained from NCVAE at
254 Belsize Road, London N.W.6. As well as issuing a monthly magazine,
which includes reviews of material useful for assemblies, they issue catalogues of visual aids. Part I covers Scripture topics, but others deal with
geography and civics, and will be found to be useful.

Where assemblies are being planned for younger children on the subject
of animals the following organisations can be approached for assistance.

National Council for Animal Welfare, 126 Royal College Street,
    London N.W.1
People's Dispensary for Sick Animals, PDSA House, South Street,
    Dorking, Surrey
Royal Society for the Prevention of Cruelty to Animals, 106 Jermyn
    Street, London S.W.1
The Royal Society for the Protection of Birds, The Lodge, Sandy,
    Bedfordshire.
Universities Federation for Animal Welfare, 8 Hamilton Close, South
    Mimms, Potters Bar, Herts

Most art galleries now make available slides of paintings and other works
of art at modest prices. Some, like the National Gallery in London,
issue large catalogues of these aids. For each festival occasion in school,
e.g. Easter or Christmas, these slides can be projected with great effect
alongside children's original writing, prose or poetry extracts, movement
work, electronic and experimental sound etc.

For assemblies involving small numbers of children, a dramatic poster
can be used. An extensive catalogue of these is available from Argus
Communications, 89 Railway Street, Hertford. For large quantities the
pro rata is lowered considerably, and a 'parish' of schools may like to
combine in the purchasing of a set which can be circulated.

Another source of picture and poster material is St. Paul Book Centre, 57 Kensington Church Street, London W.8. (Titles include — Hands, Nature Speaks, The Senses, Friends and Present Day Pictures).

# 2 MATERIALS FOR USE IN ASSEMBLIES

## BOOKS OF ASSEMBLIES

It is recommended that readers examine these books either as Inspection Copies, or at R.E. Centres or Exhibitions, to decide how far they are 'in tune' with the approach adopted by the various authors. Often only a part, and perhaps just a small part of a book will be valuable to a particular teacher. If several of the staff are engaged in regular assemblies, then it will be useful to have a wide range of resources available.

Barnett, L.: *Good Times With God* (Hodder and Stoughton)
Brimer, J. and S.: *A Morning Assembly Book* (Blackie)
Bryant, J. and White, D.: *Well God, Here We Go Again* (Hodder and Stoughton)
Bullen, Anthony.: *24 Assemblies for Juniors* (Mayhew-McCrimmon)
Campling, C. and Davis, M.: *Words for Worship* (Arnold)
Dickinson, F. and Worsnap, R.I.: *Primary School Assembly Book* (Macmillan Educational)
Dingwall, R.: *Assembly Workshop* (Darton, Longman and Todd)
Faulkner, R.: *Assemblies for Infants* (Mayhew-McCrimmon)
Frost, B. and Wensley, D.: *Celebration* I Pentecost, Trinity, Harvest, All Saints; 2 Advent, Christmas, Epiphany; 3 Lent, Good Friday, Easter Day, Ascension (Galliard)
Godwin, E.B.: *Child of God* (Religious Education Press)
Hardwick, E.: *A Theme à Week* (Schofield and Sims)
Hobden, Sheila: *Explorations in Worship; Further Explorations in Worship* (Lutterworth)
Holt, B.S.: *Looking for Meaning* (S.C.M. Press)
Jones, C.M.: *Worship in the Secondary School* (R.E.P.)
Kitson, M.: *Infant Praise* (O.U.P.)
Leicester Education Authority: *Gathered Together* (O.U.P.)
Lloyd, R.H.: *Assemblies for School and Children's Church: More Assembly Services* (R.E.P.)

Mullen, Peter: *Assembling* (Arnold)

O'Brien, Irene: *Themes of Worship* (Blackwell)

Ovens, M.: *Themes and Prayers.* (Macmillan Educational)

Patson, S.G.: *Assemblies for Primaries* (Religious Education Press)

Pinfold, F.: *The Meeting Points Assembly Book; Meeting Points Assembly Cards* (Longman)

Prescott, D.M.: *The Infant Teacher's Assembly Book; The Junior Teacher's Assembly Book; The Senior Teacher's Assembly Book* (Blandford)

Prickett, D.: *School Assemblies for 8-13s* (Denholm House Publications)

Purton, R.: *Day by Day* (Blackwell)

Swann, M.E.: *Sing and Pray (Infants)* (Blandford)

Taylor, Dorothy, J.: *Explorations in Assembly With Children* (Lutterworth)

Tressider, E.: *Worship with 11-14 Year-olds* (Chester House)

Wetz, Peter and Walker, P.: *Celebrating Together* (Darton Longman and Todd)

White, P.A.: *Dramatic Assemblies* (R.E.P.)

Wills, Elizabeth: *School Assemblies for 5-7's* (Denholm House Press)

*Together for Festivals:* Church Information Office

*Together for Harvest:* Church Information Office

*Together for Christmas:* Church Information Office

*Wider Horizons* (British Humanist Association, 13 Prince of Wales Terrace, London W8 5PG)


See also:

Schools Council Integrated Studies: *Exploration Man* (O.U.P.)

Schools Council Project on Religious Education in Primary Schools: *Discovering an Approach* (Macmillan Education)

## DRAMA

Anouilh, J.: *Becket* (Eyre Methuen); *The Lark* (Eyre Methuen)

Cawley, A.C.: *Everyman and Medieval Miracle Plays* (Dent)

Eliot, T.S.: *Murder in the Cathedral* (Faber)

Franklin, A.: *Seven Mystery Plays* (O.U.P.)

Fry, Christopher: *Boy With A Cart* (Muller); *The Firstborn; A Sleep of Prisoners* (O.U.P.)

Hussey, M; *The Chester Mystery Plays* (Heinemann)

Obey, Andre: *Noah* (Heinemann Educational)

Purvis, J.S.: *The York Cycle of Mystery Plays* (S.P.C.K.)

Rose, M.: *The Wakefield Mystery Plays* (Evans)

## STORY MATERIAL

Some of the most successful assemblies are those in which stories are read or more frequently told. Here is a short list of stories that you might like to use. Some are short enough to tell at a single session while others can be serialised. School and local librarians will be able to add to this list to provide suitable themes for stories to tell or dramatise.

Andersen, Hans Christian: *The Ugly Duckling* (Child's Play)
Bloom, F.: *The Boy who Couldn't Hear* (Bodley Head)
Buckley, H.E.: *Grandfather and I* (World's Work)
Burningham, J.: *The School* (Cape)
De Jong, Meindert: *The Wheel on the School* (Puffin)
Fanshawe, E: Rachel; *In a Wheel Chair* (Bodley Head)
Gag, W.: *Gone is Gone* (Puffin)
Grabianski, J.: *Androcles and the Lion* (Dent)
Gydal, Monica and Danielson, Thomas: *When Olly Went to Hospital; When Olly had a little brother; When Olly's grandad died; When Olly saw an accident:* (Hodder and Stoughton)
Hazen, B. and Ungerer, T.: *The Sorcerer's Apprentice* (Methuen)
Hoban, R.: *Bedtime for Francis; A Baby Sister for Francis* (Puffin)
Hutchins, P.: *Titch* (Puffin)
Keats, E.J.: *The Little Drummer* (Bodley Head)
Keeping, Charles: *Joseph's Yard; Shaun and the Carthorse; Alfie and the Ferryboat* (O.U.P.)
Krasilovsky, P.: *The Shy Little Girl* (World's Work)
Lapsley, S.: *I Am Adopted* (Bodley Head)
Larsen, H.: *Don't Forget Tom* (A. & C. Black)
*Pedlar of Swaffham* (BBC Jackanory Series)
Peter, D.: *Claire and Emma* (A. & C. Black)
Peterson, P.: *Sally Can't See* (A. & C. Black)
Roberts, P.: *David and his Grandfather* (Puffin)
Sen, F.: *My Family* (Bodley Head)
Showers, P.: *The Listening Walk* (Black)
Southall, Ivan: *Ash Road* (Angus and Robertson)
Steinbeck, John: *The Pearl* (Heinemann Educational: Pan)
Whitney, A.M.: *Just Awful* (Collins)
Wilde, Oscar: *The Selfish Giant* (Kaye & Ward)

## SPECIALLY FOR ASSEMBLIES

Carr, F.: *101 School Assembly Stories* (Foulsham)
Kossoff, David: *Bible Stories* (Collins)

Morton-George, Paul: *Stories for 8-11's* (Denholm House Press)
Petts, S.E.: *Modern Parables* (H.E. Walter Ltd, Worthing)
Prescott, D.M.: *Stories for the Junior Assembly; Further Stories for the Junior Assembly; Stories for Middle School Assemblies; Stories of Great Lives* (Blandford)
Smith, Aubrey: *Stories for All Seasons* (National Christian Education Council)
Tatlock, R. (Ed): *Stories and Prayers at Five to Ten* (Mowbray)
Wolfel, Ursula: *The Light and the Dark* (Lutterworth Press)

## BOOKS OF READINGS WITH A RELIGIOUS BACKGROUND

Banyard, E.: *Word Alive* (Belton Books)
Crellin, V.: *Tongues of Men* (Hutchinson Educational)
Daffern, T.G.: *Poems for Assemblies* (Blackwell)
Doubleday, R.: *Readings, Books I and II* (Heinemann)
Garnett, E.: *The Wheel* (Search Press)
Gollancz, V.A.: *A Year of Grace; From Darkness Into Light* (Gollancz)
Greene, B. and Gollancz, V.: *God of a Hundred Names* (Gollancz)
Hadfield, John: *A Book of Beauty* (Hamish Hamilton)
Huxley, A.: *Perennial Philosophy* (Chatto & Windus)
Laurie, R.: *Scenes and Ideas* (Evans)
Naismith, A.: *12,000 Notes, Quotes and Anecdotes* (Pickering and Inglis)
O'Brien, Irene: *Poems of Worship* (Blackwell)
Prescott, D.M.: *Poems for the School Assembly* (Blandford)
Sansom, Clive: *The Witnesses* (Methuen)
Shah, I.: *The Exploits of the Incomparable Mulla Nasrudin* (Pan)
Thompson, Denys: *Readings* (C.U.P.)

## BOOKS OF READINGS ON SELECTED THEMES, NOT NECESSARILY RELIGIOUS

There are of course many other anthologies that teachers will use, and selections from them will be great use in assemblies. There are a number of specialised collections that are useful when particular themes are being explored. The Thimble Press, Lockwood Station Road, South Woodchester, Stroud, Glos. publish a Poetry Book List.

Berg, Leila: *Four Feet and Two* (Puffin)
Cass, J.: *The Patchwork Quilt* (Longman)
Lines, M.: *Tower Blocks; Poem of the City* (F. Watts)

There are several collections of war poems, for example:

Parsons, Ian: *Men Who March Away* (Chatto and Windus)

A very useful book to have at one's elbow when preparing assemblies where a poetic element is desirable, is Helen Morris' *Where's That Poem?* 2nd Edition (Blackwell)

Look out for interesting collections of writings prepared for other situations, for example:
Clements, Simon; Dixon, John and Strata, Leslie: *Things Being Various; Reflections* (O.U.P.)
Fowler, Robert S.: *Themes in Life and Literature* (O.U.P.)
Inglis, Fred: *The Scene* (C.U.P.)

## BOOKS OF PRAYERS
Bacon, C. and M.: *Praying with Beginners* (Chester House)
Barclay, W.: *Epilogues and Prayers* (SCM Press); *Prayers for Young People* (Collins); *Prayers for the Christian Year* (SCM Press)
Batchelor, M.: *The Lion Book of Children's Prayers* (Lion Publishing)
Boyd, M.: *Are You Running With Me, Jesus?* (Hodder and Stoughton)
Buckmaster, C.: *Give Us This Day* (ULP)
Burke, C.: *Treat me Cool, Lord; God is for Real, Man; God is Beautiful, Man* (Fontana Religious)
Griffin, G.: *Praying With Seniors* (Chester House)
Hedges, S.G.: *With One Voice* (R.E.P.)
Holloway, B.W.: *Prayers for Children* (ULP)
Lynch-Watson, Janet: *A·Patchwork Prayer Book* (Hodder and Stoughton)
Martin, Nancy: *Prayers for Children and Young People* (Hodder and Stoughton)
Prescott, D.M.: *An Infant Teacher's Prayer Book* (Blandford)
Quoist, Michel: *Prayers of Life* (Gill and Macmillan)
Swann, M.E.: *Sing and Pray* (Blandford)
Webb, Joy: *This Praying Thing* (Hodder and Stoughton)
Wilton, D.R.: *Praying With Primaries* (Chester House)
Young, J. and E.: *Praying With Juniors* (Chester House)

## HYMNS AND SONGS FOR ASSEMBLIES
Adams, S.: *Sixty Hymns for Juniors* (Schofield and Sims)
Bailey, J. and Metcalfe, M.: *New Life* (Galliard)

Baughen, Michael: *A Youth Praise* (Falcon Books)
Bennett, G. and Tearman, J.: *Hello World* (Galliard)
Brace, G.: *Something to Sing at Assembly* (C.U.P.)
Briggs, E.: *The Daily Service* (O.U.P.)
*BBC Hymn Book* (O.U.P.)
Carter, Gordon: *Raise Your Voices* (Mayhew-McCrimmon)
Clifton, Geoffrey: *A Junior Hymn Book; Sing It In The Morning* (Nelson)
*Come and Praise* (B.B.C.)*
Gilbert, Bryan: *Gospel Songs for the Guitar* Vol I and II (Marshall, Morgan and Scott)
Hodgetts, Colin: *Sing True* (R.E.P.)
Kitson, Margaret: *Infant Praise* (also in i.t.a.) (O.U.P.)
Lewis, P., Lawrence, R. and Simpson, G.: *Sing Life, Sing Love* (Holmes McDougall)
Maxwell-Timmins, Donald: *Morning Has Broken* (Schofield and Sims)
Poston, M. and Holbrook, D.: *The Cambridge Hymnal* (C.U.P.)
Oswin, Sister M.: *Let God's Children Sing* (G. Chapman)
Rolls, R.: *Everybody Sing* (BBC)
Rose, M.E.: *The Morning Cockerel Hymn Book* (Hart-Davis Educational)
Solly, H.: *Hear Us Heavenly Father* (O.U.P.)
Smith, Peter and Boyce, June: *New Orbit* (Galliard); Smith, Peter: *With Cheerful Voice* (A. & C. Black); *Faith, Folk and Festivity; Faith, Folk and Clarity; Faith, Folk and Nativity* (Galliard)
Swann, Donald: *Sing Round The Year* (Bodley Head)
Tillman, June and Brailey, B.: *New Horizons* (Galliard)

---

*Also available as a cassette, 2CM 317

# 3 RECORDS AND MUSIC

**SONGS FOR ASSEMBLY ON RECORD**
*What A Wonderful World* Louis Armstrong
*I Believe* The Batchelors
*Blowing in the Wind* Peter, Paul and Mary (Warner WEP 6114)
*If I Were A Rich Man* (from *Fiddler on the Roof*) (MFP 113 1)
*If I Ruled The World* Harry Secombe (Philips AL 3431)
*The Other Man's Grass Is Always Greener* Petula Clark (NSPL 18282 Pye)
*We Shall Overcome* Joan Baez (Vanguard VSD 6560)
*Let My People Go* Paul Robeson
*A World Without Love* Peter and Gordon
*He Was My Brother* Paul Jones
*Thank You Very Much For The Aintree Iron* The Scaffold
*Thank You Very Much* (sung by Albert Finney in *Scrooge)*
*Rhythm of Life* from *Sweet Charity*
*Thank You* Petula Clark
*Where Have All The Flowers Gone?* Peter Seeger (CBS 6308)
*Food* from *Oliver!* (Decca LK 4359)
*Universal Soldier* Donovan (Pye NEP 26219)
*I Am A Rock; The Sounds of Silence* Simon and Garfunkel


**STORIES AND ILLUSTRATIVE MATERIAL ON RECORD**
*God's Brainwave* Bernard Miles (Decca ACL 324)
*Unusual Things* John Rae (BBC REC 68M)
*Ten To Eight* Andrew Cruikshank (BBC REC 043M)
*Church Bells* (BBC REC 77M)
*Bible Readings* James Mason (*Stars on Sunday* - York BYK 704)
*Jewish Chronicles* (From Jewish Folk Poetry - Heilor 2549 007)
*Gospels in Scouse* (Xtra 1058)
*The Christmas Story* (Pilgrim JLP 117)
*The Hopwood Family* (BBC RESR 9)
*Stories for Assemblies* Johnny Morris (BBC RESR 14)
*The Book of Ruth* (Caedmon TCE 111)
*The Story of Noah* (HMV 7 EG107)

*Readings from the Bible* (Garden of Eden, the Fiery Furnace,
　Noah's Ark, David and Goliath) (Brunswick LAT 8275)
*Strange Stories from the Bible:* The Case of the Unwanted Body;
　The Angry King; (Livingstone SSB 151); The Case of The
　Wealthy Pauper; The Proud General (SSB 152); The Case
　of the Men on the Roof; Deceitful Daughter (SSB 153); The
　Case of the Frightened Sailor; The Fiery Furnace (SSB 154).
*The Psalms* 8, 23, 84, 88, 91, 100, 121, 130, 149, 150
　(Caedmon TCE 115)
*The Spoken Bible Series* (NEB Series, Leomark Records)
*Martin Luther King* (Mercury DY 99256)
*Jacob* David Kossoff (EMI SEG 8331)
*Choral Verse from Alex Franklin* (with book - Oliver and Boyd)
*Samson & Ruth* David Kossoff (Pilgrim King KLPS 58)
*Adam & Eve: Tobias and the Angel* David Kossoff (Pilgrim King
　KLPS 59)

## MUSIC ON RECORDS

*Amazing Grace* (Atlantic K 60023)
*A Tribute to Youth Praise* (Key Records KL003)
*Black Nativity* (Present Records JOY 117)
*Bridge Over Troubled Water* (Simon and Garfunkel)(CBS KCS9914)
*Children Play and Sing* (Stars on Sunday—York 705)
*Faith, Folk and Clarity* (Pilgrim Recordings JLP 148)
*Faith, Folk and Festivity* (Galliard 4016)
*Folk in Worship* (BBC REC 58M)
*Frost and Fire — A Calendar of Ceremonial Folk Songs* (Topic
　127136)
*Glory to God* (Decca SKL 5049)
*Godspell* (Music for Pleasure MFP 5271)
*Golden Vanity* (Children's Crusade) (Decca SET 445)
*Gospel Songs and Spirituals for Little Children* (Music for Pleasure
　MFP 1350)
*Great Choirs* (Stars on Sunday)(York 705)
*Harvest Thanksgiving* (Tower CLM206)
*Hi Neighbour* Vol 1 (Peerless PRCC104)
　　　　　　　Vol 2 (Peerless PRCC105)
*Hymns and Songs* (BBC RESR 22)
*Jesus Christ Superstar* (MKPS 2011/2)
*Missa Luba* (Philips BL 7592)
*More Folk in Worship* (BBC REC 176)
*National Guide Festival of Song* (BBC RESR 127S)

*New Life by Good News* (RESR 29S)
*O Happy Day* (Marble Arch MALS 1152)
*Reflections on Hymns of Our Time* (RL 303)
*Simon and Garfunkel's Greatest Hits* (CBS–KL31350)
*Sing Along With The Girl Guides* (BBC RESR67M)
*Sing Praises  1*  (Cambridge Hymnal Material) (EMI ASD   2290)
          *2*                                   (EMI CSD   3598)
*Sing True* (Marble Arch MAL 1199)
*Songs Are For Singing* (BBC RESR 18)
*Songs for Assembly* (BBC RESR 15)
*Songs for Saints and Sinners* (Tower CLM 201)
*Songs of Faith and Doubt* – (Donald Swann) (Argo)
*Songs of Praise for Young Folk* (BBC RBT 21)
*Sympathy* (C & B Records CB 179)
*The Rope of Love* – (Donald Swann) (Galliard 4022)
*The Three City Four* (Decca LK 4705)
*The Trumpet of the Lord* (Regal SRS 5030)
*Twentieth Century Folk Mass* (Oriole MG 20019)

## PIECES OF MUSIC SUITABLE FOR ASSEMBLIES

Bach, J.S.: *Air on a G String; Jesu, Joy of Man's Desiring; Sheep May Safely Graze; Wise Virgin's Suite*

Bax, Arnold: *Tintagel*

Beethoven, Ludwig: *Symphony No. 6; Egmont Overture; Leonora Overture No. 3; Moonlight Sonata*

Berlioz, Louis: *Roman Carnival; Symphonie Fantastique; Childhood of Christ*

Bizet, Georges: *Jeux d'Enfants*

Borodin, Alexander: *In the Steppes of Central Asia; Polovstian Dances; Nocturne*

Brahms, J.: *Variations on a Theme of Haydn*

Britten, Benjamin: *The War Requiem; Noye's Fludde; The Fiery Furnace; St Nicholas*

Clarke, Jeremiah: *Trumpet Voluntary*

Coates, Eric: *Three Elizabethan Suites*

Copland, Aaron: *Rodeo; Appalachian Spring*

Daquin. Louis Claude: *Le Coucou*

Debussy, Claude: *La Mer. Nocturnes*

Delius, Frederick: *Brigg Fair; On Hearing the First Cuckoo in Spring; La Calinda; Hassan*

De Sévérac, Déodak: *The Musical Box*

Dukas, Paul: *The Sorcerer's Apprentice*

Dvorak, Antonin: *Slavonic Dances; New World Symphony; Symphony No. 4*
Elgar, Edward: *Wand of Youth Suite; Enigma Variations. Cockaine*
DeFalla, Manuel: *Three Cornered Hat*
Gershwin, George: *Rhapsody in Blue*
Grainger, Percy: *Shepherds Hey*
Grieg, Edvard: *Peer Gynt Suite; Piano Concerto No. 1; Holberg Suite*

Handel, G.F.: *Royal Fireworks Suite; Water Music; Queen of Sheba Overture; The Messiah*
Haydn, Joseph: *Toy Symphony; The Creation*
Holst, Gustav: *The Planets; The Hymn of Jesus*
Humperdinck, Englebert: *Hansel and Gretel*
Inglebrecht, Désiré: *La Nursery*
Khachaturian, A; *Sabre Dance*
Kodaly, Zoltan: *Hary Janos*
Mendelssohn, Felix: *Midsummer Night's Dream; Italian Symphony; Fingal's Cave*
Mahler, Gustav: *Fifth Symphony*
Menotti, Gian-Carlo: *Amahl and the Night Visitors*
Mozart, Wolfgang: *Overture to Figaro; Cosi Fan Tutte; Exultate Jubilate; Eine Kleine Nachtmusik*
Mussorgsky, Modeste Petrovich: *Night on a Bare Mountain; Pictures at an Exhibition*
Offenbach, Jacques: *Orpheus in the Underworld*
Prokofiev, Serge: *Peter and the Wolf; Love of Three Oranges; Classical Symphony; Lt Kije*
Quilter, Roger: *Children's Overture*
Ravel, Maurice: *Bolero; Mother Goose Suite. Daphnis & Chloe*
Rimsky-Korsakof, Nicholas: *Scheherazade; Sadko. Russian Easter Festival Overture*
Rossini, Gioacchino: *William Tell Overture; Silken Ladder; Italian Girl in Algiers; Boutique Fantasque; Semiramide*
Saint-Säens, Camille: *Carnival of the Animals; Samson and Delilah*
Schönberg, Arnold: *Moses and Aaron*
Smetana, Frederick: *Ma Vlast, Vltava*
Sibelius, Jean: *Valse Triste; Karelia Suite*
Stravinsky, Igor: *Rite of Spring; Firebird*
Tchaikovsky, Peter: *1812 Overture; Swan Lake; Nutcracker Suite*
Vaughan-Williams, Ralph: *Antarctica; Wasps Overture; Greensleeves; Hodie*
Walton, William: *Crown Imperial; Façade; Belshazzar's Feast*
Weinberger, Jaromir: *Schwanda the Bagpiper*